Writing Instruction K – 6:

Understanding Process, Purpose, Audience

Jan Turbill & Wendy Bean

Foreword by Mem Fox

Richard C. Owen Publishers, Inc.
Katonah, New York

Library of Congress Cataloging-in-Publication Data

Turbill, Jan.
  Writing instruction K-6 : understanding process, purpose, audience /
Jan Turbill, Wendy Bean ; with a foreword by Mem Fox.
    p. cm.
    Summary: "Describes a model for teaching writing with a focus on audience, purpose, and genre, defines good writing, examines the process of writing, presents historical changes in teaching writing, and includes assessment and professional development activities"—Provided by publisher.
    Includes bibliographical references and index.
    ISBN-13: 978-1-57274-748-7 (pbk.)
    ISBN-10: 1-57274-748-X (pbk.)
  1. English language—Composition and exercises. 2. Language arts (Elementary) I. Bean, Wendy. II. Title.
    LB1576.T87 2006
    372.62'3—dc22

2005036127

Richard C. Owen Publishers, Inc.
PO Box 585
Katonah, NY 10536
914-232-3903; fax 914-232-3977
www.RCOwen.com
Acquisitions Editor: Darcy H. Bradley
Production Manager: Kathleen A. Martin
Copy Editor: Amy J. Finney

Printed in the United States of America

9   8   7   6   5   4   3   2

Dedicated to

My friend and mentor, Bob Walshe, who believed I could write and taught me not only to write but to love teaching it!

JT

My mother, Joy, who through her constant letter writing has taught me, my sisters, and now her grandchildren the pleasures and purposes of writing.

WB

Table of Contents

Foreword

Australia is held in high esteem for its excellent standard of literacy. Its enviable reputation has not arisen overnight—it has been built up over a generation by many superb teachers and university researchers, among whom are Wendy Bean and Jan Turbill. Both are dear friends of mine, from whom I have learned a great deal. Over the years we have shared ideas, rage, laughter, passion, and hope about literacy and its teaching, in particular the teaching of writing.

This book is filled with hope. Its vast but focused aim is to restore *purpose* and *audience* to the writing curriculum in every elementary classroom. Its theories are crystal clear, and it provides practical ideas and strategies that will assist not only those teachers who sense that they have recently lost their way in the teaching of writing, but also teachers who feel that they had never found their way in the first place.

While most elementary teachers read for pleasure and read with confidence, far fewer write for pleasure or write with confidence. This has led to teachers wrongly defining "writing," let alone being able to define the difference between good writing and bad. For too long the writing curriculum has focused on the surface features of writing: handwriting—good and bad—for example, or spelling—good, bad, and passable. Many children and their teachers accord a disproportionate weighting to handwriting and spelling without realizing that it is possible to write with beautiful calligraphy and perfect spelling and yet to write appallingly.

The assumption that writing is merely getting the correct words neatly on to the paper ignores the fact that there are three dimensions to writing: the word level, at which many teachers stop and never venture any further; the sentence level, which includes a look at grammar and some punctuation; and the whole text level, which is the most relevant level, since its focus is genre and ultimately the all-important *meaning* of a piece. These levels of writing are amply and ably explored in the early chapters of this book.

In the English-speaking world there are currently four broad approaches to the teaching of writing: first, the "skills-and-drills" approach, which is still in vogue in many classrooms even though it belongs to a bygone era; second, the more wishy-washy "creative writing" approach, in which the surface elements of writing tend to be ignored (foolishly) in favor of what the child is trying to say; third, the "process" approach, which misinterprets some of the best research of the 1970s and 1980s and treats writing as a step-by-step formula, even though writing clearly *is* a real process for any writer, including me; and finally the approach that gathers all the best theories and understandings together: writing as a social process.

This last definition of writing is the foundation on which this book rests. The authors' explorations and research have led them to an understanding that writing is only real and can only be produced to the best of a writer's ability if the social *purpose* for the writing is clear, the social *audience* for the writing is known, and the response from that audience is eagerly anticipated and cared about.

Throughout these pages, in every chapter, the words *purpose* and *audience* assume a kind of mantra. This comes as no surprise to a writer like me since I would never dream of typing anything, or putting pen to paper, without a purpose and an audience in mind.

Although purpose and audience are the twin secrets to writing well, they are too often absent from our classrooms. When teachers complain that children cannot write, or are unwilling to write, let alone to draft and re-draft their writing, purpose and audience are usually the keys to making that happen.

The authors of this book guide us toward a more authentic writing classroom. Their surprising insights and gorgeous anecdotes and their sound theories and their very practical suggestions on how best to teach writing will help all of us to grow as writers first, and then as teachers of writing. Such is the wealth of their combined experience that Wendy Bean and Jan Turbill are very explicit about organizing for the teaching of writing and even more explicit about the assessment of it. While the skills-and-drills approach makes "writing" easy to assess, it does nothing to prove that children can write well, at length, or for real reasons. The assessment strategies outlined in this book ensure that children's progress is closely monitored, that they are treated as individuals with varying strengths and weakness that must be attended to, and that accountability will not be compromised.

Teachers who want fresh air in their writing curriculum, as well as success for themselves and for their young writers will be as inspired as I have been by this easy-to-read book and its quietly revolutionary message.

Mem Fox

Acknowledgments

We have had the privilege of working closely with wonderful mentors over the past two decades who have taught us so much about the teaching and learning of writing. These wonderful friends and colleagues include Bob Walshe, Brian Cambourne, Don Graves, Ken and Yetta Goodman, Don Holdaway, Andrea Butler, and Mem Fox.

We want to thank the writers of the *Frameworks* professional development program, Brian Cambourne and Andrea Butler (not forgetting that Jan Turbill was an author). We have drawn on their work for the sections on modeled writing and peer proofreading.

We wish to acknowledge that the first section in Chapter 2 has been taken directly from pages 11 to 20 of Andrea Butler and Jan Turbill's *Towards a Reading-Writing Classroom* (1984) and used with the permission of the authors and Primary English Teaching Association, Sydney, Australia.

The teachers and their students who have welcomed us into their classrooms over many years have taught us so much about the teaching of writing. We thank you all.

We would like to thank all the children who have shared their writing with us. In particular we thank the staff and students at Our Lady of Perpetual Succour, West Pymble. It was almost impossible to select samples of writing for this book, as the quality of all the writing was excellent. The teachers should feel very proud of their part in promoting literacy in this school, as should each and every student!

Family members were never safe from our excitement about their writing efforts. We thank them all, especially our nephews Andrew, Christopher, Sam, Damian, Timothy, and Matthew for what you have taught us about writing.

Our editor and colleague, Darcy Bradley, has given us wonderful support and wise advice throughout the production of this book. We thank Darcy for making sure we never gave up!

We believe in teachers and effective teaching and it is that belief that informs the position we have taken in this book. If you are an experienced teacher, we hope that you will enjoy our stories and the student writing and that these challenge your thinking and teaching. If you are beginning as a teacher, we hope that you will be inspired by our experiences to become a teacher who loves to teach writing.

Chapter 1: Teaching Writing

Over the past years we have heard so many teachers tell us, "I love to read, but I don't write much." If we continue the conversation, we find that most teachers read for pleasure and to find information. However, few ever write for pleasure, and most only write extended sustained text when they "have to." Further, teachers generally feel confident about the teaching of reading, and the resources available to them for this teaching are overwhelming. A walk around the exhibits at any literacy conference clearly demonstrates the current colorful and attractive reading programs and the recently published children's literature. Research articles on all aspects of reading fill the academic journals each year, whereas articles on writing and the teaching of writing are rather rare. In summary, it is fair to say that a focus on reading and the teaching of reading receives a great deal of attention, time, and finances.

But what of writing and the teaching of writing? Where does writing "fit" in the literacy curriculum? We know many teachers don't choose to write for pleasure; they don't feel confident about writing themselves, let alone teaching it. We also know from preparing for this book that there is little research carried out each year in the area of writing and its teaching and while whole conferences are dedicated to reading, we are yet to find the equivalent in writing.

Writing, we therefore argue, is the poor cousin of reading. It is not only the poor cousin; it seems it is also the feared cousin. Many teachers in our writing workshops share with us that as soon we ask them to write they are overwhelmed with anxiety that in some cases is quite debilitating. Often referred to as the "red pen syndrome," these teachers recall getting essays back from teachers that were covered in red pen marks. One teacher's comments seem to best encapsulate the impact that high school writing had on her:

> I used to quite like writing in my elementary school. But
> at high school and university we only ever wrote to show
> what we knew. In other words, writing was always some

form of test. So when my essays and papers came back with red marks all over them, I slowly began to believe I couldn't write. In fact I became really anxious every time I had to start to write anything new. It was like I was being personally attacked. Yet I love to read and really enjoy getting inside good writing.

Peter Elbow points out nothing can be read unless it was first written and suggests that we need to be putting *writing* before reading in our literacy curriculum when he says: "The expression 'writing and reading' violates the habitual rhythm of our tongues. We usually say 'reading and writing' so it sounds like I'm putting the cart before the horse. But I call *writing* the horse" (Elbow 2004, 9).

Five-year-old Helen agrees with Elbow. Helen had written a series of letters on her large piece of paper. It was Day 1 at school and the teacher had given all 28 children a large sheet of paper and colored pencils. She had asked them to write a story to show their caregivers when they went home. When the teacher came to Helen's table, she commented, "How clever, Helen. Read me what you have written today."

"Oh, you will have to read it. I can only write yet," Helen responded (see Turbill 2003 for details).

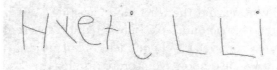

Figure 1.1: Helen's writing

Donald Graves was instrumental through his research in the late 1970s and 1980s in demonstrating that young children like Helen indeed can and do write before they read (see Butler and Turbill 1984; Calkins 1983; Clay 1975; Graves 1982; Harste, Woodward, and Burke 1984; Turbill 1982, 1983). Young children write more easily than they read because they write what they can say. While this writing may be considered immature, it *is* writing, and young children engage in it, readily making up their spelling as they go (Bean and Bouffler 1987; Cambourne and Turbill 1987). So what is it that happens in the school years that tends to de-emphasize writing and create so many people who not only don't feel confident about their writing but indeed become quite anxious when asked to write?

WHAT IS WRITING?

When we focus our attention on what constitutes writing, we find we must do so from the perspective of first considering what writing is, that is, what writing involves, and then we need to reflect on the purpose that this writing serves in our daily lives. Such considerations in turn lead us to ask: what is "good" writing and what makes it "good?"

These considerations we believe are critical if we are to be effective teachers of writing. Furthermore, we believe that to be effective teachers of writing, we need to understand how writing is related to reading, to talking and listening, and to language and literacy overall. With this in mind, a foundation upon which we might consider writing specifically, is that, "what is common to every use of language is that it is meaningful, contextualised, and in the broadest sense 'social'" (Halliday 1969, 26).

For writing to be meaningful, it must contain an inherent purpose to which the writer can relate and the reader can engage. For writing to be contextualized, it must acknowledge the reality of both the writer's and the reader's social, cultural, and political contexts that frame the writing and consequent reading. For writing to be social, it must accept the burden of responsibility that exists as writers communicate and interact with readers.

A simple definition of writing then is that writing is composing meaning into texts (using print, visual, and/or hypermedia systems) for a particular purpose and a particular audience. The interplay between audience and purpose determines the linguistic choices a writer must make, which in turn shapes the particular type or genre of writing, be it a report, narrative, office memorandum, exposition, and so on.

In addition, we believe that writing is life empowering to the extent that it affects one's participation in society, and so it must also be a lifelong endeavor as it serves to shape one's individual attitudes and behavior, and in turn shapes one's understanding of what it truly means to "write." The following comments made by the illiterate students cited by Paolo Friere highlight the life-empowering qualities of writing: "I want to read and write so I can stop being the shadow of other people. No longer part of the mass, but one of the people" (Friere 1976, 50).

Furthermore, Donald Graves reminds us that: "Children want to write. They want to write the first day they attend school. This is no accident. Before they went to school they marked up walls, pavements, newspapers with crayons, chalk, pens or pencils ... anything that makes a mark. The child's marks say, 'I am'" (Graves 1982, 3).

Writing as life empowering is very evident in this short cameo.

3

Cameo: The Power of Writing

Four-year-old Sam had spent almost an hour building a cubby house in the living room using chairs, blankets, and pillows. He crawled in and out, creating small nooks or "rooms." At times he stood back to admire his work, chattering away to himself throughout the whole process. Finally he announced, "Nearly finished." With one last task to complete, Sam took the notebook and pencil from the phone table and sat and wrote a series of signs. These he stuck to the blanket with tape at various places. The signs read "cEp awt!! NO gls ulwd" (Keep out! No girls allowed!), "trsp wil B shot!!" (Trespassers will be shot), and "Ole dady can enta" (Only Daddy can enter).

The writing was meaningful to Sam, as it had an inherent purpose of keeping out the females in his life. It was contextualized. It related to Sam's social reality, including the literature that was read to him. He informed his father that his cubby needed signs so "Mummy, Nanna, and Aunty Jan know only boys can come in." And he added "Owl has signs outside his house, too!" a reference to *Winnie the Pooh* by A. A. Milne (1926). It was social because Sam knew he would have readers for his writing and he expected that his readers would understand not only the content of his messages but also their purpose and respond accordingly. No one told Sam that he had to spell the words correctly. No one taught him handwriting lessons before he was allowed to write. He simply wrote it because he understood the *power of writing*.

In summary, we believe that writing is a social and cultural practice that is multidimensional.

WRITING AS A SOCIAL MULTIDIMENSIONAL PRACTICE

As young Sam demonstrates, writing a text that is meaningful and appropriate for the context and fulfills the purpose for readers draws on multiple dimensions or levels of understandings and skills. These we can refer to as the "word level," "sentence level," and "whole text level." The following figure is intended to be three dimensional in order to demonstrate how all three levels interconnect in order to compose effective or "good writing,"— that is, writing that achieves its purpose for its intended audience.

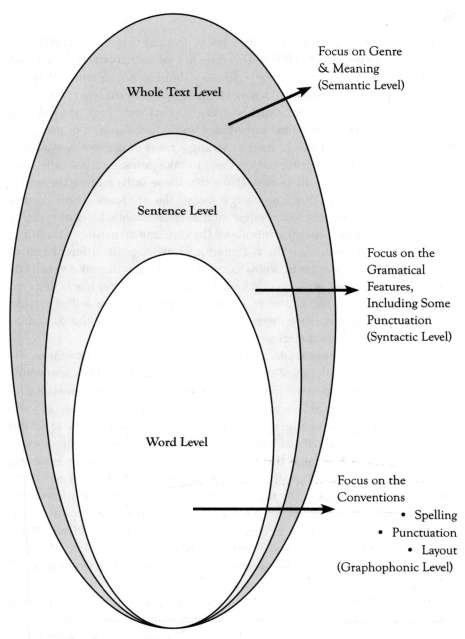

Whole Text Level

Focus on Genre
& Meaning
(Semantic Level)

Sentence Level

Focus on the
Gramatical
Features,
Including Some
Punctuation
(Syntactic Level)

Word Level

Focus on the
Conventions
• Spelling
• Punctuation
• Layout
(Graphophonic Level)

Figure 1.2: Writing as a social multidimensional practice

Whole Text Level

Writers write best about what they know. Donald Graves (1982; 2004, 89) continually reminds us of this fact. This does not mean that our students must always choose their own topics or write only about topics on which they are already "experts." However, it does mean that if we want students to write on certain topics we need to make sure we have helped them "build the field" so that they have developed some knowledge and understanding of the topic. We need to teach our students, be they young writers or university students, how to find appropriate information, how to take notes, and basically how to make the information their own. (Note that these skills require the writer to also be a reader). This knowledge forms the students' "background knowledge" or "semantic knowledge" and is the semantic level of writing. We also need to teach our students about the different structures of writing; how they can communicate their semantic knowledge in different genres of writing. Without semantic knowledge, the writing will make very little sense, and it becomes obvious to an audience that the writer has little or no knowledge on the topic. However, even with semantic knowledge, writers need to be able to structure their writing so that it achieves the particular purpose for the intended audience.

For instance, eight-year-old Stevie knew a great deal about snakes. He knew the different varieties of snakes that inhabit Australia. He knew which ones were harmless and which ones were poisonous. He knew how to safely capture them and how to look after them in captivity. Yet when asked to write a science report on snakes, he was stumped. He did not know how to set out a report, how it began, about topic sentences, about writing in the present tense, and so on. Writing at the whole text level therefore means knowing not just the information, but also how to structure the information across the whole text--what to put in the first paragraph, how to order the information in the following paragraphs so that the flow of the information unfolds in a logical sequence, and how to conclude. In other words, in addition to his background knowledge on snakes, Stevie needed background knowledge of the genre of report writing. He needed to be able to use a particular genre of language to achieve a particular social function.

A genre is therefore a particular form of language that has particular features and is used to achieve a particular purpose. Buying something over the telephone requires us to use a "shopping" genre; writing to the editor may require us to write in the genre of "letter of complaint"; writing a report on snakes requires knowledge of the genre of "science reports." The flow of meaning across the sentences, the cohesive ties, the references, and the choice of appropriate vocabulary all become very important if the final writing is going to represent meaning for the reader at the whole text level.

Sentence Level

Writing at the whole text level so that the meaning unfolds in a logical manner requires the writer to be able to structure one sentence after another. Knowing the grammar (or the syntax) of the language is necessary for each sentence to carry the required meaning. This involves word order, subject-verb agreement, use of plurals, appropriate use of tense, and so on. Writers need an understanding of the syntax of language that allows them to choose the grammatical features at the sentence level that are needed to both carry the meaning and to develop the required genre. Some knowledge of punctuation also operates at the sentence level.

Word Level

Writers also need to focus on the word level. They need to know relevant vocabulary, how to spell these words, and how to punctuate. These aspects are often referred to as the conventions or mechanics of writing, and they too carry meaning, but in the main this meaning operates at the word level. For instance, in the sentence "I found Penny's hat" we know from the capital *P* and the apostrophe *s* of "Penny's" that the meaning of the word is a person's name, not coins. When we read on to the next word, "hat," our meaning at the word level and sentence level is confirmed. Equally as important is that writers can revisit their writing and proofread it carefully in order to identify unconventional spellings and then be able to write the conventional form.

Having discussed what writing is and that it involves multidimensional skills and understandings, let's turn our attention to what constitutes "good writing." How do we know when writing is "good" or effective?

WHAT CONSTITUTES "GOOD" OR EFFECTIVE WRITING?

There is no simple answer to this question, but when a group of eleven- to twelve-year-old children were asked the question at the annual Meanjin writers' camp in 1985, they agreed that "good writing" was writing that wasn't boring. It was the kind of writing that holds the reader's attention, whether it is fiction or nonfiction.

Many teachers of writing have tried to answer this question. Fox and Wilkinson identify some 22 indicators of "good writing." Each is explored with useful examples in their book. We have chosen a few examples to list:

- Good writing keeps the reader in mind
- Good writing is clear writing
- Good writing flows from paragraph to paragraph
- Good writing has well-crafted endings
- Good writing has been revised (Fox and Wilkinson 1993, 4-8).

Macrorie reminds us that "good writing" doesn't waste words, is convincing, and arrests the reader's attention.

. . . [M]ost good writings gain their power in these ways:

- They don't waste words
- They speak in an authentic voice
- They put readers there, make them believe
- They cause things to happen for them [readers] as they happen for the writer (or narrator)
- They create oppositions, which pay off in surprise
- They build
- They ask something of readers
- They reward them with meaning (Macrorie 1985, 34).

These lists seem to be rather predictable and would most likely correspond to what the general community might say when asked to respond to the question "what is good writing?" However, it is a very different list from the responses a group of teachers gave to the same question. Day's research, the results of which are shown in Figure 1.3, found that a group of over seventy Grade 2 teachers in some 35 New South Wales schools ranked the ability to use correct spelling and punctuation as the top two criteria for what constitutes "good writing" in their classrooms (Day 1999, 75). It is our experience that many teachers today would respond similarly.

Criterion	Percentage
Spelling and Punctuation	35%
Sentence Structure/Grammar	16%
Imagination/Creativity	14%
Appropriate Genre	11%
Sequencing of Ideas	6%
Handwriting	6%
Vocabulary	6%
Editing	4%
Length	1%

Figure 1.3: Key indicators of "good writing" stated by Grade 2 teachers (Day 1999, 75)

These findings are a concern to us and hence one of the reasons for this book. We want all teachers, particularly teachers of the early years, to understand that writing is life empowering and needs to be meaningful, contextualized, and social to learners as they move from nonwriters to writers of print-based, visual, and hypertexts. It is more than spelling and punctuation. We especially want children to continue to *want* to write as they move through their schooling, to feel confident in their writing, and to know that writing is life empowering.

While we acknowledge that these mechanical skills are important and need to be learned, we also believe that such a strong focus on these "skills of writing" as indicated by the teachers in Day's research is a recipe for turning children away from being confident writers who actually enjoy writing.

Therefore, we believe strongly that teachers of writing need to take time to explore the important question: What is good writing? What makes writing "good?" Not only do teachers need to make explicit their criteria for what they perceive "good writing" to be, but they also need to articulate these to their students. Teachers need to understand that while they may not feel confident as writers nor confident in teaching writing, they can give their students messages in many implicit ways about what they perceive constitutes "good" writing and in particular what good writing "looks like" with respect to their students' writing. These criteria also tend to become the assessment framework used when judging their students' writing. In turn these often implicit expectations impact on their students' view of themselves as writers and attitude to writing overall. In what follows are two short cameos that clearly demonstrate this.

Cameo: "A School Story or a Real Story?"

Some years back on a wet Sunday afternoon Jan was minding her then six-year-old nephew, and he was bored! She suggested to him that he use the computer to write a "story." Chris was excited about this idea and sat himself at the computer. He was about to start but stopped to ask, "Will I write a school story or a real story?"

Jan was thrown by this question, so she quickly asked, "What is a school story? What does it look like?"

"Well," he said, in a matter-of-fact tone, "you know—it goes: I am a...; I live in a...; I eat..."

Jan quickly replied, "No. Write a real story." And with that Chris wrote a narrative full of invented spellings about "The Trip to the Moon." He stopped occasionally to re-read it and to share with Jan and his brother Andrew. He didn't worry about his spelling. When he finished, he wanted to read and re-read it.

9

> ### THE TRIP TO THE MN MOON
>
> One day dad said do you, want to go to the moon? Yes I said just as Andrew was geting the roket redy. It is time for cout don so we did —ten nine eight seven six five four three two one lift of we have lift of. As we went parst planet Pluto I saw a monsta on the planet. Andrew said Why don't we land there. I said yes it is a good idea So we did. When we landed we desited to tack the bugy and whepons on the planet. I was the one caring the whepons and Andrew rode the bugy out of the secret drivewy. I conected the laser bems to the bugy and stuk the flaf in the grand. We trided to shoot the lazer beem but we coud not shoot it. We were so scard that we ran back to the ship and tryd to tack of but the monsta held us down with his long tentikuls. I said Wie don't we put on full pouwer. We are yelled Andrew. The monsta broke in and we were terfid. It started to eat our heads off .... In 1 or 2 minits .... THAT WAS THE END OF THE STORY.....

What Chris called a "school story" reflected the expectations that his teacher gave about "good writing" for six-year-old children. Further questioning established that the teacher wrote these "stem" sentences on the board, and the children had to choose their own animal and fill in the gaps. Furthermore, the children were expected to copy the words from the board in neat handwriting and all spelling was to be "correct."

On the other hand, outside of school Chris perceived "good writing" to be an adventure that was full of action. It had an introduction, a series of happenings, and to quote Chris, "was good to read."

Cameo: "I Can't Spell Too Good."

We were both at a Riverina Children's Writers Camp. The two-day workshops were run at a site beside one of Australia's largest and longest rivers, the Murray River. Mark was in Grade 6 in what is called in Australia a "one-teacher" school. His school was in an isolated rural town also on the Murray River. His teacher had sent him to the writers' camp because he was the only Grade 6 child in his small school of nine students.

During the two days Mark had spent most of his time playing with his fellow writers rather than doing much writing. On this day he was told he had to spend the morning writing before he could go and play tennis. We observed Mark take his clipboard and sit at the base of a large gum tree and write. About ten minutes later he was standing beside us, clutching his board against his chest. When asked to read his writing, he held it close so we couldn't see it and read it aloud.

> The reeds so life-like and incomparable
> The water so swift and deadly
> The mud so putrid and sticky
> The undergrowth so rugged and vast
> And all of this is the magnificence of nature

We were stunned. Such a powerful piece of writing, written so quickly!

"It's not very good," Mark quickly added.

"What makes you think it is not very good?" we asked, noting he was still clutching the clipboard to his chest and not letting us see it.

"'Cause I can't spell too good," he said. We eventually pried the clipboard from him and yes, there were many spelling errors, but we pointed out to Mark these did not detract from the powerful writing he shared with us. He grinned and ran off to play tennis.

Figure 1.4: Mark's poem

Mark's perception of "good writing" from his school experiences was that "good writing" must be spelled correctly.

Both cameos clearly indicate teachers' expectations and echo Day's (1999) findings. So how can we help teachers create criteria for what they perceive to be good writing that are more in line with Fox and Wilkinson and Macrorie?

CREATING CRITERIA FOR "GOOD WRITING"

Shelley Harwayne suggests that among the knowledge that teachers need is "considerable expertise in knowing what makes good writing" (2001, 150). She notes that all members of a school faculty should be well informed about the qualities of good writing and suggests ways of prompting staff to talk about good writing.

We have also found in the many workshops we offer to teachers that if we move the teachers' focus on "good writing" away from their classroom practice, they begin to identify quite different criteria for what they consider to be "good writing." Such criteria are more in line with those that professional writers list as discussed above. In one workshop we ask teachers to identify a piece of "good writing" and to respond to the question: "What makes the piece 'good?'" We ask them to bring along an excerpt from children's literature that they claim is "good writing." After a general discussion about published writing, we ask the teachers to move into groups of four to five and share with each other their respective excerpts. Some read their excerpt aloud and others bring along copies for their peers to read. The purpose of the group is to identify what "makes" the respective pieces of writing "good." When talking about narratives, teachers identify criteria such as storyline, strong and plausible characters, great dialogue, clear descriptions, a plot that "grabs," appropriate use of adjectives and adverbs, strong verbs, and many other aspects. When focusing on information texts, they identify criteria such as suitable headings, a clear topic sentence, clear information set out in reasonably short, concise sentences, use of present tense, appropriate terminology, use of visuals to support the information, and so on.

What also becomes apparent during the group discussions is that some of the linguistic choices that a writer has used so effectively violate the very "rules" that teachers teach their children. For instance, in the opening paragraph of Chapter 3 of *Charlotte's Web,* E. B. White writes:

> The barn was very large. It was very old. It smelled of hay and
> it smelled of manure. It smelled of perspiration or tired horses
> . . . It smelled of grain and of harness dressing and of axle
> grease and of rubber boots and of new rope. And whenever
> the cat was given a fish-head to eat, the barn would smell of
> fish. But mostly it smelled of hay . . . (1952, 18).

Our teachers always agree that this paragraph is a great piece of writing. It conjures up the most wonderful images and sometimes not-so-wonderful smells. And it does so through the appropriate use of short and long sentences, through repetition of "it smelled," and the use of "and ... and ... and" as well as through the use of such devices as beginning a sentence with "And," followed by one beginning with "But." Our teachers admit that while they tell their students they *cannot* do these things, White does and does so very effectively. So our next question is: "Why does it work so well for White?" When teachers begin to respond to this question, they begin to "get inside" White's linguistic choices and to identify their own criteria.

After teachers have explored several excerpts of writing from books of well-known authors that they love to read to their classes, their criteria for "good writing" grow. After such a workshop we ask the teachers to carry out a similar set of activities with their class in order to create a composite criteria list so that the students have the same insights and shared understandings as their teachers. In this way both teachers and their students are learning about the connections between what is read and what can be written. They learn about how to write from what they read. They are making connections between reading and writing.

Chapter 2:   Reading-Writing Connections

We began this book discussing how we often refer to writing in conjunction with reading. The reading-writing connections, or what Peter Elbow (2004) would call the writing-reading connections, seem obvious at one level. However, just how reading serves writing is a question worth exploring in detail. Once teachers have a deep understanding of the responses to this question, it is our experience that they are more able to help their students also understand the reading-writing connections.

HOW DOES READING SERVE WRITING?

In 1984, Andrea Butler and Jan Turbill wrote a book entitled *Towards a Reading-Writing Classroom* that focuses on the reading-writing connections. One particular chapter in this book, "The Reading-Writing Processes," seems as pertinent today as it was then. We have revised relevant parts to reflect our current thinking. However, much is the same and we do not apologize for that. The concepts are as important today for our teaching of writing as they were in 1984.[1]

We begin with the questions:

- What are the similarities between the reading and writing processes and how do these "fit" within the language arts context?
- What does a reader learn about writing from reading?
- What does a writer learn about reading from writing?

Many opportunities exist in the reading classroom to make connections to writing. Reading and writing are both acts of composing. Readers, using their background knowledge and experience, compose meaning from the text; writers, using their background knowledge and experience, compose meaning into text. For both processes it is helpful to look at what readers do

---

[1] Much of this section is taken directly from Andrea Butler and Jan Turbill's *Towards a reading-writing classroom*. Rozelle: Primary English Teaching Association and Portsmouth, NH: Heinemann, 1984, pages 11-20.

in each of the three different phases: before the act of reading and writing, during the act of reading and writing, and after the act.

What Readers Do *Before* Reading	What Writers Do *Before* Writing
The proficient reader brings and uses knowledge: • About the topic (semantic knowledge) • About the language or syntax used (syntactic knowledge) • About the sound-symbol system (graphophonic knowledge). The proficient reader brings certain expectations to the reading cued by: • Previous reading experiences • Presentation of texts • The purpose for the reading • The audience for the reading.	The proficient writer brings and uses knowledge: • About the topic (semantic knowledge) • About the language or syntax to be used (syntactic knowledge) • About the sound-symbol system (graphophonic knowledge). The proficient writer brings certain expectations based on: • Previous writing experiences • Previous reading experiences • The purpose for the writing • The audience for the writing.

Copyright © 1984 by Andrea Butler and Jan Turbill.

Figure 2.1: What readers and writers do before reading and writing

What readers do before reading and writers do before writing is shown in Figure 2.1. The expectations and prior knowledge that readers and writers have will predetermine how they will approach future reading and writing tasks. The reader has expectations and begins to make predictions, based on prior knowledge and experiences, presentation of the text, and visual cues. The purpose for the reading becomes clarified and the desire to continue to read increases or decreases based on these expectations. For example, a reader expects a newspaper to have certain types of information arranged and presented in a certain way. These expectations are based on the types of newspapers the reader has read before. Newspapers are organized differently according to their scope and subject area, their purpose, and their audience. For instance, a daily national newspaper differs from a local county newspaper and both will differ if presented on the Internet rather than in paper-based form. A financial paper will differ from a sports paper; both will be different again in magazine form.

Readers make reasonable predictions about the expected content, style, and format of these materials and choose what they will read in depth, skim over, or ignore. A simple example is when we pick up our daily mail. The logos on the envelopes and the fact that the address has been typed or hand written begins us making predictions about the "meaning" within the envelope and just how much "reading attention" we might give to its contents. If we recognize the logo of our telephone company, we expect the contents to be a monthly bill. Once opened, we might choose to read only the amount to be paid. If this amount is not what we expect, we then may choose to read the contents more carefully, trying to make sense of the information having difficulties with, we might choose to ignore or discard the envelope unopened. We go through a similar process whether we are choosing a book to read, an article we need on the teaching of writing, a new recipe, and so on.

These expectations have been formed by readers over time as they experience a wide range of texts read for a variety of purposes. It needs to be pointed out also that not all these expectations may be positive. Many of us develop negative expectations about reading certain types of texts, and some develop negative expectations about reading any text at all.

The writer will likewise have expectations as to how a text might develop and will begin to consider questions such as:

- Why am I writing this?
- Who will be the reader(s)?
- How do I structure my writing, i.e., What genre do I use? Should the text be a list, a report, a narrative?
- Do I know enough about the topic? Do I need to talk to someone or read more about the topic?

These decisions will be made by the writer based on past experiences as well as considering the purpose and audience for the writing to be undertaken. For example, if we are writing a shopping list for ourselves, we will not be too concerned about spelling or handwriting. However, if we are writing the list for a friend who has volunteered to do the shopping, not only might we give more care to the handwriting and spelling, but we also might need to be more specific regarding the information in the list as to amount, brand, and so on.

In many real-life situations, both readers and writers can decide to continue or simply give up at this stage, depending on their purpose, interest, and motivation. However, for our students this is not an option. Therefore, we need to make sure that what happens before reading or writing is motivating and engaging. We need to convince our young learners that being able to write and read effectively is life empowering, so it is imperative that we make sure the task at hand is purposeful, interesting, and achievable.

What Readers Do *During* Reading	What Writers Do *During* Writing

The proficient reader is engaged in:
• Draft Reading
  - skimming and scanning
  - searching for sense
  - predicting outcomes
  - defining and composing meaning
 	
• Re-reading
  - re-reading parts as purpose is
    defined, clarified, or changed
  - taking into account, where
    appropriate, an audience
  - discussing text; making notes
  - reading aloud to "hear" the
    message
 	
• Using writer's cues
  - using punctuation to assist
    meaning
  - using spelling conventions to assist
    meaning
	The proficient writer is engaged in:
	• Draft writing
	  - writing notes and ideas
	  - searching for a way in, a "lead"
	  - selecting outcomes
	  - revising and composing meaning
	
	• Re-writing
	  - re-writing part of text as purpose
	    changes or becomes defined or
	    clarified
	  - considering readers and the
	    intended message
	  - discussing and revising text
	  - re-reading to "hear" the message
	
	• Preparing for readers
	  - reading for correct punctuation
	  - proofreading for conventional
	    spelling and meaning
	  - deciding on appropriate
	    presentation

Figure 2.2: What readers and writers do during reading and writing

The table in Figure 2.2 lists and compares what readers do during reading and what writers do during writing. Draft reading and writing can be defined as the "refinement of meaning which occurs as readers and writers deal directly with the print on the page" (Tierney and Pearson 1983, 571). Like every writer, what every reader needs is a first draft—an opportunity to "have a go" at working on the text without fear of being wrong:

> A reader opens his or her textbook, magazine, or novel;
> a writer reaches for his or her pen. The reader scans the
> pages for a place to begin; the writer holds the pen poised.
> The reader looks over the first lines of the article or story
> in search of sense of what the general scenario is . . . The
> writer searches for the lead statement or paragraph to
> the text . . . Once [the scenario is] established the reader
> proceeds through the text, refining and building upon his
> or her sense of what is going on; the writer does likewise
> (Tierney and Pearson, 1983, 571).

What Readers Do *After* Reading	What Writers Do *After* Writing
The proficient reader: • Responds in many ways, e.g., talking, doing, writing • Reflects upon it • Feels success • Wants to read again.	The proficient writer: • Gives to readers • Gets response from readers • Feels success • Wants to write again.

Figure 2.3: What readers and writers do after reading and writing

Figure 2.3 lists what readers and writers do after reading and writing. While these tables may be over-generalized, they do serve to highlight the reading-writing connections. Considering the processes in this way demonstrates the many implications for the teaching of writing and reading. What also becomes apparent is that neither the reader nor the writer can exist without a text. Writers must produce them and readers must interpret them. Texts always stand between the two and can be a bridge or a barrier to meaning. As Frank Smith reminds us: "Text is a two-sided mirror rather than a window, with writers and readers unable to see through to each other but gazing upon the reflections of their own minds." (1982, 87).

If a reader is to receive the intended message about particular content, the writer must follow certain conventions (Smith 1982). These conventions are more than surface features of the text. They are embedded in the text at the whole text, sentence, and word levels. They include all those features that make one text different from another—a novel different from a street directory; a poem different from a recipe.

CONVENTIONS AT THE WHOLE TEXT LEVEL

Presentation and Layout

Different types of texts are organized and presented according to the content matter, purpose, and audience. A telephone book is presented in a very different layout from a cook book or a novel. Therefore, it is also read differently. Websites have opened up very different ways of presenting information. Young children learn to read these sites and navigate their way around them with relative ease.

Genres

Different subject areas, purposes, and audiences require different forms or genres of writing. For example, a novel is written in a different genre from a science report; an e-mail to a friend about a conference is in a different

genre from an e-mail to the Dean of Education requesting
in order to attend a conference.

Cohesion

Different genres bring into play different cohesive ties. Senten
across paragraphs are knitted together into a meaningful whole te
the use of these ties. In the earlier excerpt from *Charlotte's Web,* E. B. White
uses repetition of words such as "it smelled of," each "it smelled" clearly
referring to the barn. Such repetition carries meaning across the whole text.
Vocabulary chosen, such as "smelled," "manure," "perspiration," "tired
horses," "fish-head," and "hay" connect in readers' minds across sentences
to build meaning about this barn in such a way that for many of us we can
literally smell the barn. The use of referential pronouns such as "it" also carry
meaning across the sentences at the whole text level. We know as readers that
"it" refers to the same "barn" mentioned in the very first short sentence:
"The barn was very large."

CONVENTIONS AT THE SENTENCE LEVEL

Certain conventions are expected at the sentence level. These tend to fall
into the category of grammatical or syntactical knowledge. Most punctuation
also tends to operate at the sentence level. Knowing what constitutes a
sentence in English and that it needs a capital letter at the beginning and a
period (or full stop) at the end are very important conventions at the sentence
level (and as most of us have experienced very difficult to define easily for
our students). Use of dialogue and how to punctuate it is another. The use
of grammatical features such as subject-verb agreement, use of strong verbs,
use of adjectives and adverbs, passive or active voice, tense, plurals, and
clauses and their order in the sentence and phrases are all conventions that
operate at the sentence level. How and why sentences are structured in the
way that they are depends on what is required at the whole text level in order
to achieve the genre and its purpose for the intended readers.

CONVENTIONS AT THE WORD LEVEL

Word level mostly involves the choice of specific vocabulary and
conventional spelling of that vocabulary. Again, the choice of vocabulary and
its spelling is contingent upon the content of the writing, its purpose, and the
intended readers.

WHAT DOES THIS MEAN FOR TEACHERS?

Frank Smith suggests that we certainly cannot learn all three levels (whole text, sentence, and word) and these connections through didactic teaching. "What is learned is too intricate and subtle for that, and there is too much of it. There is just not enough time" (Smith 1983, 561). He proposes that it is mainly through reading that writers initially learn all the techniques they know or need to know. To know how to write for a newspaper one must read newspapers; to write poetry one must read poetry. "Children," Smith suggests, "must read like a writer, in order to learn how to write like a writer" (1983, 562). Likewise, Shelley Harwayne writes that teachers learn about good writing by listening to experts talk about texts, by reading professional books about how to "craft" writing into a successful final product, and from listening to each other (2001, 150).

Smith believes that when we read like a writer we are consciously aware of the way that the author has written the piece. It is rather like the Saturday social golf players watching professionals in action. Because the watchers also play golf, they are more capable of appreciating the skill and finer points of style than people who have never played golf and who have no interest in the game whatever. The weekend amateur players who are having difficulty with their swing, putting techniques, and so on know how hard it is and so watch carefully at how the professionals do it. They actively engage in the demonstrations before them and are highly motivated to practice the observed play.

In the same way, learners who regard themselves as writers will engage in the written texts that they read differently from learners who do not write. As they read they seem to be able to "get inside" the author's head and appreciate the conventions at the whole text, sentence, and word levels that the author uses to create the particular text to achieve a particular purpose for readers. Smith suggests that what is happening is that: "The author becomes an unwitting collaborator. . . . Bit by bit, one thing at a time, but enormous amounts of things over the passage of time, the learner learns, through reading like a writer, to write like a writer" (Smith 1983, 564).

However, Smith is quick to add that we do not read like writers every time we read. He points out that this will not occur when the attention of the reader is overloaded trying to work out the inherent meaning in the text, when the reader is focusing on "getting it right," as when reading aloud, or "when we have no expectation of writing the kind of written language we read" (1983, 563). To read like a writer we must do so in a special way. First, we must perceive ourselves to be writers. We must also see the need to write the type of text we are reading. Finally, we need to read in a way in which we engage with the author as a collaborator, that is, get inside the head of the author.

Thus we believe that if learners perceive themselves as writers and in particular writers of a certain text, they are going to be more likely engaged in the language conventions of that text more readily. They will read the text as potential writers of that text. Furthermore, everything our students read and everything we read to them are demonstrations of the written language that they as writers can draw on.

One last important point we need to make here is that many avid readers will not necessarily be avid writers. However, they do have the potential to become avid writers given the appropriate conditions. On the other hand it is unlikely for those who don't read to ever become avid writers.

Creating a classroom community in which our students want to write is the challenge of all teachers from kindergarten to Grade 12. It has always been a challenge for teachers to find the "best approach" to the teaching of writing. We hope that the remaining chapters help teachers in this challenge.

Chapter 3: Revisiting Approaches to Writing Instruction

A search of the many teacher resources and the Internet will identify hundreds of different "approaches" to the teaching of writing. In fact, in preparation for writing this chapter, we put "approaches to teaching writing" into Google™ and received over 2,000,000 hits in two seconds! We found the "product approach," the "process approach," the "creative approach," the "heart of wisdom approach," the "six traits approach" and the "six traits+1" and even the "do it wrong approach," just to name a few. Five broad groups emerge from our reading, our own research, and personal experiences that describe the teaching of writing since the early 1960s. Each group roughly aligns with a decade, but this does not mean that the focus of one group disappeared as it moved into the next decade (see Figure 3.2). These groups can be labeled:

- Writing as production
- Writing as creativity
- Writing as process
- Writing as a social process
- Writing as a tool for thinking and learning.

These groups may seem arbitrary, but we feel they serve the important purpose of being able to view some of the basic theoretical assumptions that have underpinned the various approaches to the teaching of writing both past and present. You may be able to add to the few examples we will discuss here. We are also very aware that many approaches overlap our grouping.

WRITING AS PRODUCTION

"Writing as production" is characterized by the view that reading, writing, spelling, and grammar are disparate skills that can be taught separately. The major teaching focus is on the word and sentence levels, with the belief that if components of these levels are correct then the whole text level will also be correct. These beliefs were predominant in classrooms up until the mid 1960s (and are still evident in many classrooms today). Some may refer to this approach to teaching as traditional, skills-based, or structural.

A focus on writing as production saw the ability to spell the most frequently used words in English and the ability to handwrite neatly as necessary prerequisites to being able to compose meaning into written form. Therefore teachers believed that children needed to learn to spell and handwrite at a basic level before they could begin to write. The very term "writing" tended to be synonymous with handwriting, while the term "composition" was used for what we now simply call "writing" in the elementary school. (It should be noted that the term "composition" is still often used at the college level.) It was also believed that basic punctuation and grammar skills should be taught explicitly to students in decontextualized lessons, often from textbooks or exercise sheets or computer software. It followed that once these skills were mastered, students would transfer the skills they had learned when they actually came to write connected text.

Another characteristic of writing as production is that students need to be given the topic and ideas for writing. This tends to be particularly so for the very young children who were, and in many classrooms still are, given simple topics such as My Pet, My Favorite Toy, and so on.

A major belief inherent within the this approach is that once students have been taught basic knowledge of spelling and handwriting and grammar, they are expected to remember all these skills, consider the topic, organize their ideas, and write a one-shot piece of writing; a piece of text that is to be correct in all ways: meaning, spelling, handwriting, grammar, and punctuation. Little or no time is given to revision or proofreading. These compositions are usually collected and graded by the teacher, then returned to the students. Errors in grammar, spelling, and punctuation are pointed out to the students, often in red pen. The expectation inherent in such practice is that the students will learn from having the errors exposed to them. It is interesting to note that the time given for composition was usually a weekly time slot of about one hour, whereas spelling, punctuation, and grammar exercises were often given daily time and tested regularly.

We believe that such a strong focus on learning the skills or mechanics of writing is driven by a view of learning that suggests that learners are not capable of learning unless someone more expert—the teacher or the textbook—breaks that which is to be learned into small, isolated "bits" and teaches these to inexperienced learners in a predetermined order. The learners practice them and are tested on them, and only when each bit is mastered can they move to the next bit. This view of learning is based on a behaviorist theory of learning (Skinner 1957), a theory that is still inherent in many teaching approaches today.

Crossing the Line from Traits to Product

There is a danger that teachers who hold a behaviorist view of learning will implement current approaches, such as Six Traits and Six Traits + 1 approaches (Culham 2003; Spandel 2000), in a formulaic way (Conner 2003). These two approaches advocate that there are six key traits that writers need to attend to. The traits can be seen to operate at the whole text, sentence, and word levels when the teacher uses them as an overall framework that can guide the teaching of writing. Conner, a Grade 4 teacher, carried out research in her classroom with her students. She used these six traits as a guide to teach her students to self reflect on their writing and therefore to want to revise it.

Conner then summarized the traits as she used them with her students:

1. Idea Development: the writing is clear and supported by the kind of detail that keeps readers reading
2. Organization: the order of the piece guides the reader through the text
3. Word Choice: natural language paints a strong, clear, and complete picture in the reader's mind
4. Voice: the writer's energy for the subject; makes the text lively, expressive, and engaging
5. Sentence Fluency: an easy flow makes the text a delight to read aloud
6. Conventions: the writer shows excellent control over standard writing conventions and uses them with accuracy and creativity to enhance meaning (2003, 70).

Conner's research indicated that the six traits could be used by students to assess their writing as well as to work with their peers in order to revise and edit their writing. However, she also found that these traits were only one aspect of her overall writing program. Understanding the important role that audience and purpose play in the development of writing as well as understanding that the teaching of writing needed to happen at the whole text, sentence, and word levels were vital additional aspects in her classroom practice. Conner warned that if traits are treated as skills or steps to be taught and practiced in isolation from each other, then such teaching will tend to fall into writing as production approach.

We continue to encounter classrooms today in which practice demonstrates that the teachers' focus is still very much on writing as production. These teachers present skills in writing as separate entities that need to be taught, practiced, and assessed by them. Jan's memories of teaching writing with a strong focus on product are very clear, especially with one particular Grade 2 class that she taught in the late 1960s, as she describes in this cameo.

Cameo: Swinging on a Gate

In the late 1960s I was asked to teach a class of twenty Grade 2 children—all considered to be "remedial" readers and writers. I was also given the expectation that I would bring them "up to scratch" with the other Grade 2 children. "Composition" (as it was called) was scheduled every Wednesday for the hour between morning break and lunch. I began to hate Wednesdays. The topics for the compositions were chosen by the principal and set out week by week in advance. Her argument was that only if all second graders wrote on the same topic could she "grade" the compositions—and grade them each week she did—all 150 of them! The five "best" writers were selected by the principal to read their stories in assembly each Monday. Needless to say, it was a rare occurrence when any of my students were given this privilege.

One particular topic I recall was "Swinging on the Garden Gate." To this day I have no idea what most people could write about given this topic. But we gave it our best shot. We went out to the school gate and all had a go swinging on it to give us inspiration. We brainstormed the words we might need. I reminded them about neat handwriting and correct spelling and away they went. I ran around, bent over them (no wonder I have a bad lower back these days), writing spelling words for them and asking, "Well, what could happen next? What else could you write?" "You know Mrs. S likes to see at least a page of writing," I would add. What a nightmare. Lunchtime came and they wanted out of the room and I was exhausted. All except for Justin, who to my surprise said he hadn't finished! I was stunned. He read me his page about how he loved to visit his grandfather's dairy farm because where ever he went with Grandad around the farm, his job was to jump out and open the gate and shut the gate. And he did this by taking a big jump and swinging on the gate. It was a great piece—the first time that Justin had ever written more than a few lines. While the rest of us struggled, Justin excelled because he could make this topic his own. I learned something about writing that day. And yes, it was one of the rare times one of my students was chosen to read in assembly.

WRITING AS CREATIVITY

During the 1970s and 1980s, we began to transfer our thinking and teaching from writing as product to the teaching of writing as a creative act. Walshe defines creativity as "the drive to link up ideas, events, relationships that haven't been linked before and are in that sense original" (as cited in Foreword, Dumbrell 1997, ii). Writing, like talking, is considered creative and an expressive mode of language. The assumption that "what can be said can be written" emerged, and such thinking gave rise to the notion that we should provide many opportunities for our students to "talk their way to meaning" before asking them to write. For instance, in science, we might encourage students to observe and talk about what they see before attempting to write what they observe. The term "composition" gave way to a new term: "creative writing," a term used today to describe a particular approach to the teaching of writing.

A creative writing approach encourages teachers to set the scene in order to develop students' imagination and creativity before asking them to write. Thus teachers might play scary-type music, darken rooms, and light candles to set the scene for ghost stories, take students outside to listen to the birds in spring or observe the many different colored leaves in the fall, watch construction workers at work, and so on. Opportunities to talk about these experiences are deemed necessary so that students can begin to articulate what they might write. Vocabulary words generated by this talk are written up on charts or the board for students to use in their writing.

This approach led to considerable changes in writing instruction. However, those who advocated a creative writing approach in the 1970s and 1980s demonstrated little understanding of the connections between spelling and writing, grammar and writing, and reading and writing. In our experience some even suggested that the correction of the spelling, grammar, punctuation, and handwriting in these "creative" pieces might be detrimental to the child's creativeness and therefore should be avoided. Instead, these skills needed to be taught explicitly as separate lessons, with the belief that once they learned them, children would transfer them to their creative writing.

Today "creative writing" is a term still commonly used to describe a certain approach to the teaching of writing. A glance through the millions of hits on the Internet indicates that, in the main, this approach incorporates the notion that writing is also a process, as can be seen in the following:

> The Creative Writing Process permits the author to
> construct through a series of well planned out stages, a

thorough piece of writing that is both organised in its
presentation and thorough in its development. Since
this is a process, we are dealing with several stages of
development from the initial thoughts and ideas to the final
polished product (Kirby on http://www.nzcal.com/hp/
adk/, accessed January 2005).

Creative writing approaches seem to focus mostly on imaginative or
fictional writing to the exclusion of nonfiction, expository, and other kinds
of writing. From our reading there still seems to be little understanding of
how to incorporate the teaching of spelling, grammar, and punctuation into
the writing lesson. And rarely is clear reference made to the importance of
reading for writing.

WRITING AS PROCESS

Professional writers have always viewed writing as a process. Their ideas
come from their many experiences and observations of life around them
(Elbow 1981; Macrorie 1985; Murray 1982). And they know that the final
publication will not come from a single "sit-down-and-write-a-one-shot-
draft."

Donald Graves introduced us to the term "writing process" and what
became known as the "writing process approach." He showed us that young
children *can* write if given the opportunity, pencil, and paper (1982, 2004).
What was so special about Graves' research was that he encouraged teachers
to become researchers in their own classrooms by suggesting that they
observe what happened when they asked their students to simply "write." For
many teachers, particularly those of five to six year olds, these observations
dispelled theories before our eyes that we had held about our young learners.
Such "theories" included the idea that children needed to be taught phonics
and the spellings of words in isolation before they could possibly begin to
write connected sentences. We heard as well as saw our students unravel the
graphophonic mystery as they "invented" their spellings in their attempts
to write. Classrooms became "phonic factories" in which children were
sounding out words they wanted to write as well as helping others to do
so. Children were developing and using their phonemic awareness as they
attempted to write on topics of their own choosing.

Another critical aspect of the research during the 1980s and 1990s (Butler
and Turbill 1984; Calkins 1983; Cambourne 1988; Graves 1982; Harste,
Woodward, and Burke 1984; and Walshe 1981, among others) was the
realization of the connections among writing and spelling and reading. It
became apparent that if we wanted our young students to write, they had to

be immersed in the language of books; they had to read and be read to. We recognized that written language differed from spoken language, and so our students needed to do more than write down what they could say; they also needed to write "the language of books."

The writing process approach as espoused by Graves and others is underpinned by language theory; namely that readers and writers draw on the same language system. This system can be viewed as three subsystems that readers/writers use simultaneously to compose meaning from or into texts. They use their world knowledge or background knowledge and experiences (the semantic system). They use their knowledge of how language works— the grammar of the language (the syntactic system), and they use their knowledge of the sound/symbol relationships (the graphophonic system). As we demonstrated in Chapter 1, this knowledge is multidimensional and operates at the whole text, sentence, and word levels.

When one accepts this view it becomes clear that writers draw on the same language subsystems (namely the semantic, syntactic and graphophonic systems) and do so simultaneously as they attempt to compose meaning. Just as in reading, an overemphasis on one system at the expense of the others is likely to make the task of composing meaning more difficult than it needs to be. For instance, a strong focus on the word level, such as getting all spelling correct in a first draft, is likely to impede a writer's desire to write very much at all.

The strong focus on writing as process can be best explored in Figure 3.1 (adapted from Walshe 1981; 1999). Such a model has clear implications for classroom practice.

When teachers view writing as a process they understand the need to provide time and opportunities for pre-writing. This will include many of the activities highlighted within writing as creativity, such as providing experiences and opportunities to talk before writing. However, the "before writing" phase involves more. It means understanding that even before our students begin to write, we need to help them understand the purpose for the writing and who the intended audience might be. Teachers need to demonstrate strategies that help students access the information they need for their writing. These strategies include searching the Internet, using a library card or electronic catalog, using an index, note taking, skimming and scanning texts and websites for key words, using graphic organizers such as mind maps, and many more. What becomes clear is that writers cannot write if they do not have some knowledge of that which they are to write.

Much of this "before writing" work can occur before "writing time" in the school schedule. It may occur during library time or in science or social

BEFORE WRITING		DURING WRITING			AFTER WRITING	
Experience or Problem	Prewriting	Draft Writing	Revising and Editing	Product and Publication	Readers' Response	Writer's Attitude
• decision to write • growth of intention • focus on topic • focus on audience • focus on purpose	• incubating • conversing • reading • researching • thinking • considering appropriate genre	• writing • some revising while drafting • using "temporary" spelling	• recasting • polishing • rewriting • reconsidering purpose and audience • reconsidering conventions of chosen genre • proofreading	• choosing appropriate format • deciding on layout and presentation • dispatching to readers	• response is conveyed to the writer	• feelings • reflecting on the writing experience

Figure 3.1: Writing as a process

Process Is Not Linear, but Recursive

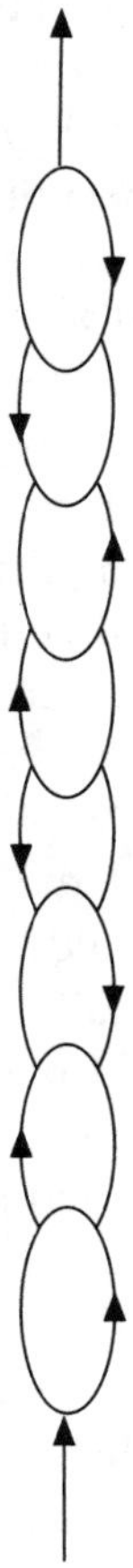

studies lessons. It may occur over a period of time. For instance, a Grade 2 class placed wheat seeds on wet cotton balls in small glass containers.

Each day they observed their respective seeds, drew them, and made a brief note about what they saw in what they called their *Science Logbook*. In science lessons they talked about seeds and their growth, and the teacher read them books about seeds—both fiction and nonfiction. Their teacher told them that they would eventually each write their own description about their respective seed's growth. Some two weeks later they began this writing. And when they did, each child had a great deal of information to use in his or her report titled: "How Wheat Seeds Grow."

The "during writing" phase means getting started on writing sustained, connected text. In the 1980s, writing drafts was a new concept for many teachers, as it meant accepting writing with many so-called errors. This was and still is very difficult for some teachers (and parents). The term "invented" or "temporary" spelling was coined to identify misspellings in drafts rather than calling them errors. Since children were being encouraged to write at the same time that they were learning handwriting skills, these drafts also often appeared to be very messy. Teachers found various ways of organizing the children's drafts. Some had children write in blank page books; some had them write on paper that was then stored in a folder.

One of the greatest challenges for teachers within this approach was helping children to "fix" their drafts: to revisit the writing to see if it made sense, to add or delete parts, and finally to proofread it. Teachers found that many times children did not want to do any more to their writing once they had written the first draft, and it was easier for the teacher to fix the spelling, grammar, and punctuation themselves than for the students to do it.

The idea of a conference was introduced as a teaching time in which the teacher worked one on one or with a small group to teach children how they might "fix" their writing drafts. The purposes of these conferences were many: to listen, to identify student needs, to guide the students in reworking their first drafts, and so on. Implementing successful conferences meant making sure that the other children were also learning. This often led to various group activities, or having helpers in the room so the teacher was able to run conferences.

The "after writing'" phase saw children's writing adorning walls in the classroom and corridors of schools. Classroom and school libraries often had sections for the "published" books of children. Children saw their writing read by others and not simply kept hidden away in a school cupboard. With the advent of computers in classrooms, published children's booklets became even more professional in their appearance. When children saw their work valued in this way, they became more willing to not only write but to edit and proofread their writing.

The "writing as a process" approach was seen by many as a revolution in the teaching and learning of writing (Butler and Turbill 1984; Cambourne 1988; Graves 1982; Walshe 1981). While there were many difficulties in implementing a "writers' workshop" within a classroom of 30 children, there were also many great successes. Two major outcomes were that children began to want to write and teachers enjoyed teaching writing! However, the strong focus on process, and the simple "fun" teachers and their students were having, often meant that understanding the relationship between purpose and audience for writing and the role this had in shaping the particular genre or text type was not made explicit by teachers.

WRITING AS A SOCIAL PROCESS

What has become clear as we explore the different approaches of the past four decades is that the teaching of writing has come a long way. It is no longer perceived to be a separate "subject" taught on Wednesday between 10:00 a.m. and 11:00 a.m. As we have moved through the years, our knowledge and understandings about writing and the teaching of writing have changed quite dramatically. Yet this does not mean that we have thrown out those key aspects that we accepted and found important in past decades. A visual representation of the changes in the understandings and teaching for writing over the years might look like the diagram in Figure 3.2. What seems to be clear is that the teaching of writing is a far more complex enterprise than it was forty years ago.

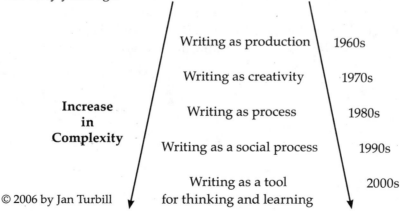

Figure 3.2: Changes over time in the teaching of writing

31

In the early 1990s we began to understand more clearly that language is indeed social, functional, and uniquely human. We use it to get our needs met and to make meaning (learn) in our worlds. We therefore use language to achieve many purposes within the contexts in which we live. To this end language is life empowering. To be effective language users means to understand the power of writing and reading and how the two serve each other. To understand the power of writing we argue that we must understand the power of writing as a social process (Delpit 1988; Derewianka 1990; Friere 1998; Harris et al. 2003; Luke 1993).

WRITING AS THINKING AND LEARNING

As we came to understand the social nature of writing, we also began to understand that writing and language are tools for thinking and learning. This means that while we may have "writers' workshop" as a set time in our daily or weekly classroom schedules, writing occurs in many parts of the students' day in and out of school. Writing no longer can be considered just a subject. It is a tool for thinking and learning. Our students need to know the skills of writing just as they did in the 1960s; they need opportunities to be creative in nonthreatening contexts as they did in the '70s; they need to understand the process of writing as they did in the '80s. But they need to know much more in order to be effective writers in today's world. They need to understand the roles that audience and purpose play in the shaping of the particular text types or genres of written language that they may need to use for the particular purposes in their lives. Teachers cannot teach students all the genres they might need in their lives today and tomorrow. However, we can teach our students to understand the principles and strategies they will need to write those genres. We can teach them that writing is a life-empowering tool for thinking and learning. The following chapters articulate what this means for the teaching of writing in our classrooms today.

Professional Development Activity: Developing a Definition of Writing for the 21st Century

In Figure 3.2, we demonstrate that over the years the teaching of writing has become more complex. We argue that writing is a social process and a powerful tool for thinking and learning. This professional development activity is useful for getting teachers to reflect on this within their own personal contexts.

Background:

1. Read Chapter 3.
2. Create an overhead of "Figure 3.2: Changes over time in the teaching of writing" or draw it on a chart.
3. Have ready blank sheets of paper, chart paper, and marker pens.
4. Allocate an hour for the activity.

Procedure:

- Explain to the group that they are going to develop a definition of writing that is grounded in today's context, and that it can become the next layer in Figure 3.2.
- Provide the instruction:
- Take a blank piece of paper and make four columns. Label the first column, "What I wrote." Label the second column, "Why I wrote it." Label the third column, "I wrote for . . ." Label the last column, "When I wrote it."
- Now reflect over the past few days and identify all the things that you wrote. This includes anything you wrote with a pen, pencil, keyboard (including cell phones and personal organizers). When you have finished this list, go back and fill in the other columns. For example, in column 1, a first item might be, "e-mail." In the second column, you might have, "to update my family on what I am up to"; "to inform a parent of a student that he has not been at school all week"; "to request an appointment with the principal" and so on. In the third column you now need to list the audience for each item, and in the last column list when (the time and place) you wrote it (15 minutes).
- Allow participants ten minutes for this individual task.
- Ask participants to form groups of three or four and share what they listed (15 minutes).
- Give out the chart paper and marker pens. Ask participants to now consider all the items they listed, the many purposes, and the audiences and contexts in which they wrote. Ask them to develop a definition of writing that includes all that they have discussed and write it on the chart paper (15 minutes).
- Post the charts for all to read.
- Ask each group to now consider what implications their respective definition of writing has for the teaching of writing. List the key points on a new piece of chart paper and post this (15 minutes).

Chapter 4: Basics of Writing and the Role of the Teacher

We believe all teaching stems from certain beliefs that each teacher holds. These beliefs are sometimes articulated and sometimes not, but they are always there. Such beliefs tend to determine the choices of strategies, resources, organization, and assessment procedures we use. Therefore it seems appropriate that as authors we make explicit our beliefs and share how these beliefs would be reflected in our teaching of writing whether our students are teachers in our workshops or children in our classrooms. We acknowledge that there is a great deal of overlap and repetition as these basics are unpacked into classroom actions. However, this only serves to illustrate the strong connections between a consistent theoretical base and its respective classroom practice.

We encourage our readers to explore their personal theory or beliefs about the teaching of writing and share with their colleagues how such beliefs are reflected in their classroom practice. When we ask teachers in workshops to do this, we find it is often easier for them to first jot down their classroom writing practices: strategies, resources, organization, and assessment procedures they use. Once these are listed each person is asked to explain why they do what they do in the name of teaching writing. These discussions begin to help teachers make explicit their beliefs or personal theories that underpin their daily classroom practice in the writing context. This activity is a very worthwhile professional learning experience.

In the next chapter, we provide a model for teaching writing (Figure 5.1). As the model is "unpacked" we describe what each of these considerations looks like in our classrooms. Finally, we describe the things the students can do to learn, apply, and develop the skills of writing and to develop a love for writing.

OUR FOUR BASICS OF WRITING

These four basics of writing are ours. We recognize that other teachers may have quite different basics. What is important is that there are strong links between teachers' basic beliefs and their classroom practice. In what follows we share our basics with our readers. We then explore each in more detail and outline what each basic belief would mean for our classrooms.

BASIC 1: WRITING IS A LANGUAGE ACT

Basic 1: Effective writers need to understand that like talking, listening, and reading, writing is also a language act and therefore draws on similar semantic, syntactic, and graphophonic knowledge.

In classrooms, this means:

- Teachers give students time for talking and listening before, during, and after writing.

Students need time to talk about their topics before they start to write. Talking and listening are used before writing with the purpose of helping the students focus and get an initial sense of audience for their writing. During writing, talking and listening can help students clarify and check for meaning and will often lead to revising and rewriting. After writing, talking and listening can be a way of getting audience response to writing as well as giving the writer a sense of satisfaction, which will lead to a desire to write again.

- Teachers take every opportunity to make links between reading and writing.

We acknowledge whenever possible the link between reading and writing. This might be during modeled writing lessons or when we read to students. Through these demonstrations and discussions we can focus on specific aspects and skills that we want students to learn. This might include how a particular genre such as an information report is structured, aspects of grammar or vocabulary, and various stylistic devices used by authors. Most importantly we want students to learn what good writing sounds like.

- Teachers support a developing awareness of the social nature of writing, in particular the notion that writing is a form of communication.

Teacher demonstrations and teacher talk can help young writers notice and appreciate the role of writing as a form of communication to oneself as well as to others. As students develop a sense of the social nature of writing, a more sophisticated knowledge of audience and purpose will evolve.

- Teachers provide opportunities for students to share the sources of their inspiration for their writing.

As young writers talk about their writing, their ideas, and even the crafting of their writing, this talk can be a source of new knowledge for other students. Therefore, many opportunities are provided for this talk to take place. Sharing sessions are short and focused, with teacher support.

- Teachers provide students with opportunities to develop content knowledge for their writing (building the field).

Semantic knowledge or content knowledge is part of the writing act. Not only do writers need control of the process of writing, but they also need to have content knowledge to engage in the writing act. This is important for writing in all genres, but particularly important when writing factual text. Give time to discuss plans for writing and to assist students in gathering content knowledge when the need is identified.

BASIC 2: WRITING IS WORTH LEARNING

Basic 2: Effective writers need to be confident writers. They need to understand that writing is life empowering and therefore worthy of learning.

In our classrooms this means:

- Teachers give students the opportunity to write every day in a supportive, risk-free environment.

While there is much to teach in the writing classroom, teachers must also give time to providing opportunities to use and practice what students are learning. Daily writing takes a variety of forms and is one of the most important parts of the writing program for students of all ages. Daily writing includes students being provided with regular opportunities to write creatively about themselves and their world. It also includes opportunities to write across all learning areas in a range of genres.

- Teachers value students' writing explicitly through sharing and meaningful feedback.

Regular writing is encouraged through quality teacher response. All writers, young and old, experienced and inexperienced, need feedback, particularly reluctant writers. Feedback in our classrooms is meaningful and responds to the writing content and form. While this feedback needs to be supportive, it also needs to be constructive and honest. Providing meaningful feedback is time consuming, but done well it is very encouraging for the writer.

- Teachers provide appropriate scaffolds to ensure success and to boost students' confidence in themselves as writers.

Writers need to feel successful. An important part of our role as teachers is to provide appropriate scaffolds for our learner writers so that they experience a sense of achievement and success. Scaffolds can take the form of students working in pairs or groups, retelling known stories, adapting existing texts, and using wall print, checklists, and other forms of teacher support as required.

- Teachers provide many opportunities for students to reflect on their writing and to share their writing with peers.

We aim to build a community of writers. Providing students with time to reflect on their own writing and to share their writing attempts with each other begins to build trust and respect for each other as writers. In such a community students feel safe to experiment in their writing, trying new ideas and new genres, as well as sharing personal insights and information. All writers in this community have much to offer each other and all writing is valued.

BASIC 3: WRITERS NEED TO UNDERSTAND THE ROLES OF AUDIENCE AND PURPOSE

Basic 3: Effective writers need to understand the roles that audience and purpose play in shaping the different types or genres of writing.

In our classrooms, this means:

- We read aloud to students (at all grade levels) as often as possible. When appropriate, we discuss the author's perceived purpose for writing and its intended audience.

Listening to a range of well-written texts helps students to hear what good writing sounds like. When reading aloud, taking one or two minutes to refer to the author's purpose for writing and intended audience is a reminder for students of the reading-writing connections.

- Students are engaged in a range of writing tasks that demand a response such as letter writing or writing via e-mail.

In our classrooms a genuine response to even a simple piece of writing is considered important. We want writers to develop a sense of audience, and this can be challenging for us as teachers. We use a number of simple ways of introducing students to audience, such as the use of a class message board where children can leave messages for each other or writing thank you notes to class visitors or helpers. We provide opportunities to publish students' writing in a range of formats wherever possible, such as in the school newsletter or on the class or school website. Sometimes, however, the purpose of the writing may be to learn how to write something in particular, such as a character description, and the audience will be self, the teacher, and other class members. Whatever the writing task, we make sure that we discuss the purpose and intended readership for the writing before we begin. Classrooms are busy places so we try to make use of the many simple measures that will reinforce audiences and purposes for writing so students learn that writing can take many forms because of the range of audiences and purposes.

- Students are regularly involved in "author's circles" or "helping circles," where they receive an oral response to their writing from their peers and teacher.

These circles are unique opportunities for students of all ages to get an initial response to their writing. Because the feedback is oral, it does not tend to focus on the surface features of writing but rather remains focused on meaning. We find that teacher modeling of this strategy is crucial, as it depends on developing good questioning and listening skills.

- Teachers always give students opportunities to talk about the purpose and audience for their writing before they begin writing.

In the same way that helping circles can assist students in getting genuine audience feedback for their writing, so too can "getting started chat groups" in the focusing stage of the writing process. Students in these group chats focus each other on their respective writing tasks, and in doing so they clarify the purpose and audience for that writing.

- Teachers make appropriate models of various genres readily available in the classroom.

Our classrooms offer many demonstrations of the various genres we want our students to learn. If we want students to learn to write a particular genre, we make sure we have a collection of books in the class library for the children to read and refer to. We read aloud to students and discuss many of these books with them. For instance, if we want students to learn how to write a science report, we explore in detail "what makes a science report?" by unpacking published examples. We think about how the author structured such texts at the whole text, sentence, and word levels. We make a criteria chart that identifies the key criteria for a science report and display this in the room. We might write a group science report, referring back to our criteria chart and modeling for our students how to structure such a report (as well as modeling the process of writing). We encourage students to draft their own science reports while referring to such charts as they write. And finally we make sure we display examples of our students' completed science reports for all to read.

BASIC 4: WRITERS NEED TO UNDERSTAND THE WRITING PROCESS

Basic 4: Effective writers need to have an understanding of the process of writing, including an understanding of why it is important to learn to spell, punctuate, and understand appropriate use of grammatical features.

In our classrooms, this means:

- Teachers regularly model all aspects of the writing process in an explicit and systematic manner.

We use modeling and teacher talk to demonstrate to students all the processes of writing, including focusing, composing, editing, and proofreading. Teacher modeling is not just about the surface features of writing but is concerned with control of the process, even with beginning writers. Engagement in all the processes requires a range of skills, so teacher modeling and instruction are important to ensure the development of these skills.

- Students are regularly reminded of the process of writing.

An outline of the writing process is displayed on a chart in the classroom in an appropriate way to meet the needs of the group and is referred to regularly. This means that students also learn a language to talk about writing. Students are encouraged and supported to plan their writing before beginning, and support continues as the young writers move through the processes of writing. Students of all ages are encouraged to take responsibility for all aspects of their writing and are supported in doing so through modeling and scaffolds.

- Teachers explicitly teach and model editing and proofreading strategies.

The skills of editing and proofreading are taught explicitly and systematically within the context of writing. Giving students the skills and language to participate in helping circles can be the beginning of the editing process whereby students begin to understand the need to revise in order to make their writing clearer and more effective.

Proofreading is concerned with the surface features of the writing and is best taught once the students become readers. Once again, we believe teacher modeling is a powerful strategy. Various approaches to proofreading are demonstrated as the writers develop. We have a proofreading guide readily available in our classrooms (see Appendix 9). The use of the overhead projector and more recent technology such as interactive whiteboards are useful tools for demonstrating and developing the skills of editing and proofreading. We use pieces of writing especially designed to make particular teaching points and therefore develop students' skills. We also provide opportunities for students to edit and proofread each other's writing. In addition, students learn how to apply the processes of editing and proofreading on the computer. Older students can learn to use the tracking tool now in word processors to make the changes resulting from proofreading and editing explicit.

- Teachers explicitly teach and model spelling strategies.

While we encourage our students to spell words the best way they can (what we like to call "temporary" spelling), we also guide our students to understand the need for correct conventions in all published work. In order for this to be successful we have a role as teachers to teach spelling strategies, which in turn become part of the proofreading process. This means firstly being able to recognize when a word is misspelled and secondly knowing how to find the correct version. Therefore our classroom needs to be supportive of the development of these spelling strategies. For instance, developing word banks of words that end, for example, in -*ough* or a list of words that are our "troublesome words" gives students reference points to check their spellings. We encourage the students to use "have-a-go" cards or books where they can practice or have a go at writing unknown or tricky words. Many resources are available to cater to the needs of the individual learners, one of the most important being a variety of dictionaries. Students are encouraged to make use of their have-a-go cards, personal dictionaries, commercial dictionaries, word lists, and other resources when writing (see Appendix 8).

APPLYING THE BASICS

The lists under each of our four basics for teaching writing are by no way complete. As we have already indicated, these basics are ours. What we have shared is not only what we believe but also how we might implement these beliefs. How these basics will look in a classroom of five year olds will differ in sophistication and complexity from how they translate into a classroom of twelve year olds. However, the same basics apply in both classrooms.

Chapter 5: A Model for Teaching Writing

Even if all teachers accept the four basics outlined here, no two classrooms will be the same. However, we have developed a model that best depicts all that we have discussed to this point. This model for teaching writing (Figure 5.1) is a practical framework for setting up classroom practice. In the remainder of this chapter we discuss each component of the model separately but remind the reader that they are interdependent.

The core of the model is *audience and purpose* and their relationship to the choice of *genre*. The interplay between audience and purpose plays a role when engaging in each part of the process of writing as well as in learning and applying the various skills related to learning to write.

Audience and purpose are also the keys to teaching the processes and skills of writing effectively. As teachers, we need to make what we know about writing much more explicit to the students we teach. Without a strong grasp of the role of audience and purpose, we can only teach students the mechanics of writing. In the end students must be able to select a genre to accommodate an audience and achieve the purpose of their writing. Because of the important role of audience and purpose across all aspects of writing and skill development, we will discuss this in more detail in Chapter 6.

The second part of the model is the process of writing that we discussed in detail in Chapter 2. The third part of the model refers to the skills required to engage in writing, such as spelling, grammar, punctuation, reading, handwriting, and computer skills. These aspects of teaching writing need to be situated in a supportive risk-free classroom learning environment that develops a community of learners.

The bottom section of the model refers to core teaching strategies that move from teacher directed and teacher control (instruction) to student directed and student control (use). These teaching strategies are modeled writing, shared writing, guided writing, and independent writing and are discussed in detail in Chapter 7.

Developing a Community of Writers

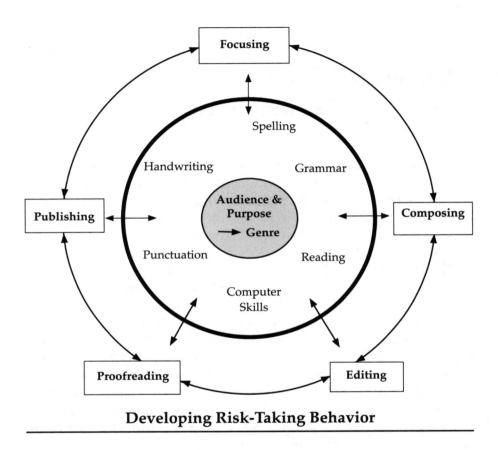

Developing Risk-Taking Behavior

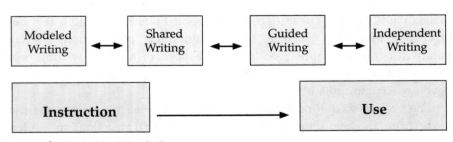

Figure 5.1: A model for teaching writing

AUDIENCE, PURPOSE, GENRE

The centerpiece for the model warrants its own chapter (see Chapter 6) to fully explore the relationship between audience and purpose and the teaching of writing. The aspects of audience and purpose are the driving forces behind any writing. They also determine the genre that will be required.

THE PROCESS OF WRITING

The processes involved in writing are shown as a recursive cycle (Figure 3.1) involving focusing, composing, editing, proofreading, and publishing attributed to Walshe (1981, 1999). Depending on your experience in the classroom this may be a very familiar cycle. In the 1980s educators came to realize that writing involved a process and that process was as important as the product. Most educators would agree this was a tremendous step forward in the teaching of writing. As we have moved forward, our understandings about the teaching of writing have been built on this knowledge.

Most teachers now accept that engaging in a process when writing is fundamental to becoming a writer. However, as we have moved our focus to genre or text types, in many classrooms the process of writing has been largely forgotten. Instead, the focus is on teaching the structure and grammar of a genre. What can result is mechanical writing that is often a one-shot draft.

This observation is supported by recent research and practice, which indicates that focusing on what students do as writers results in more effective written communication. Unfortunately, instruction in the writing process often prescribes a simple linear formula: from prewriting (generating and organizing ideas) to writing to postwriting (revising and editing). In reality, all three stages in the process are interactive and recursive (U.S. Department of Education 2001, 1-2).

Recently, when Jan asked 40 students between the ages of ten and thirteen what they thought about while they are composing, the complexity of the process becomes evident. When we analyzed the students' responses shown in Figure 5.2, we discovered they could be categorized into three general phases of the writing process. These student responses also confirm that there are no barriers between the various processes or stages of writing—that is, the writer moves backwards and forwards depending on the audience and purpose for the piece.

Prewriting	Writing/Revision	Postwriting
Feelings: anxiety, nervousness, sadness, fear, panic, criticism, confusion, hatred, blankness, humor, joy, anticipation	Write a draft Get ideas down Don't worry about spelling or punctuation yet	Give to a reader Perhaps try different readers Seek advice, help, ideas
Sense impressions: smells, sounds, pictures, fantasy pictures . . .	Pen goes fast but mind goes faster Edit, shape, tighten, expand	Decide on presentation: handwritten, computer Feel satisfied
Thinking, remembering	Re-write, thinking of audience and purpose	Perhaps want to write again
Making decisions: where to start, how to plan, will it be too personal, should I be boastful, which questions in my head will I answer, who is the reader . . .?	Proofread	What have I learned?

Figure 5.2: Students' reflections on their personal writing process

Our classrooms need to be places where this process is not only evident but also spoken about. The key teaching strategies described in Chapter 7 provide opportunities to model and teach the students the skills required to engage in each of the processes. Scaffolds or charts on display in the classroom can also be helpful, but their use will depend on the needs of the students and the understandings of the teacher.

THE SKILLS OF WRITING

Punctuation, grammar, reading, handwriting, computer skills, and spelling are identified as the skills students need as they develop into writers. As students become more experienced writers, teachers need to be prepared to teach the more complex skills required. Each of the skills is briefly dealt with below. However, to give the detail they warrant they really are the topic for another book.

Punctuation

Fox and Wilkinson define punctuation as "a written code for the sights and sounds of spoken English" (1993, 88). Therefore, punctuation is for the reader, as it is an aid to meaning. Punctuation provides the "signposts" that assist the reader to find his or her way through the words on the page. To punctuate well the writer needs a strong awareness of the intended reader. Therefore in our classrooms we:

- Take every opportunity to point out various forms of punctuation when reading and writing. Shared reading (large text) and modeled writing provide ideal opportunities to do this.
- Place short, unpunctuated pieces of student writing on the whiteboard or overhead (with permission) so the class or small group can punctuate the piece.
- Refer to books in the classroom to check on more complex punctuation, such as dialogue. For example, a teacher could say, "Let's look at what Patricia Polacco did when she used direct speech in *Thank You, Mr. Falker* (1998) when Grandpa gave Trisha her first book." If we model this type of behavior we strengthen the reading-writing connection and our students will realize that these books are models of good writing that can be referred to at any time.
- Encourage students to read their writing aloud so that they can hear where punctuation is needed. It is useful to ask students to work in pairs when doing this.
- Discuss how writers use punctuation for various effects.

Grammar

Like punctuation, grammar is for the reader. A writer needs to choose appropriate words and order them in an acceptable way. Appropriate or "correct" word order occurs in the first instance at the sentence level. Each sentence then builds and develops the meanings across the whole text levels. "Correct" grammar ensures that the writing flows and that the reader gets the writer's intended message. Grammatical choices will change according to specific genres.

Many students will come to school using sophisticated grammar in the spoken form. Much of this will be evident in early writing attempts, as these tend to be talk written down. Written language has different grammatical structures from spoken language. As with punctuation, students will learn a great deal about the grammar of written language from reading and being read to. It is also vital that much of this knowledge is taught quite systematically and explicitly within the context of the writing classroom. While students might often use correct grammatical structures in both their oral and written texts, they will not automatically have a language to talk about grammar concepts explicitly. The strategies of modeled writing and modeled reading provide wonderful teaching opportunities to demonstrate and teach various aspects of grammar. As teacher modeling proceeds in order to meet identified needs, students will begin to develop this language and therefore be able to talk about grammatical structures and features. This will develop gradually, but the teacher must consciously talk about these structures and features in meaningful contexts to facilitate the learning.

These same teaching points on conventional forms and appropriate use of grammar can be followed up within the guided writing and guided reading experiences, whether they are small group or individual sessions. These sessions or writing workshops will also be the places to teach students to use the sophisticated grammatical structures that will extend their choices as writers.

All such teaching needs to take place within the context of the writing so that it all makes sense to the students. We make no suggestion that grammar should be taught in isolated lessons but rather be taught contextually with the outcome of improving a student's use of language. As with all aspects of writing, the books the students are reading and the books you are reading to them will be their most valuable resources in exploring how words are used to meet the needs of various forms of writing.

Reading

Acts of reading and writing are difficult to separate. So much of what we can learn about writing we can learn from reading. Modeled reading, shared reading, guided reading, and independent reading times all offer opportunities to teach students about writing as we teach them about reading. If we do this well, as students read independently, they will be much more aware of written text and will often find themselves "reading like a writer."

Likewise, reading skills will develop as students write. Students will constantly find themselves reading for real purposes. However, the teacher has an important role in making this reading-writing connection explicit. Brief descriptions of the key teaching reading strategies are given to highlight the opportunities for making connections to writing.

Modeled reading

Modeled reading is a powerful teaching strategy that can be used for many purposes. Modeled reading involves reading aloud to the class daily. From time to time the teacher might stop reading and "think aloud" about the various aspects of the reading process. A variety of texts should be used in all grades, including picture books, fiction, and factual texts. Reading to students leads to vocabulary acquisition and demonstrates effective skills of reading aloud. It fosters an understanding of reasons for reading and writing and provides a time for reading for pleasure.

Shared reading (shared text experience)

Shared reading is a cooperative, supportive, reading activity with any age group, using enlarged texts such as big books, overhead transparencies, interactive whiteboards, or charts. Texts should be selected for their quality, high interest level, and particular demonstrations of how language works and to support the identified teaching focus the teacher wishes to make. Shared reading provides an opportunity to explore the author's style and skill and therefore make connections to writing. The teaching focus will be planned in terms of the group needs.

Guided reading

In a guided reading lesson, a group of students read a text that has been selected by the teacher. The teacher's role is crucial; the teacher selects the text, introduces it, and guides the students through the text. The teacher takes every opportunity to develop the skills of reading closely and analytically. Taking a few minutes at the beginning of the lesson to ask questions such as "Have a quick look through the book. What kind of text will this be (story, article, poem, and so on)? What makes you think that?" or "What audience do you think the author had in mind?" will help strengthen the reading-writing connection.

Independent reading

Within the daily literacy block there must be time for students to read suitable materials independently. A range of materials should be made available for students to practice their reading skills on familiar and unfamiliar texts at an independent reading level. From time to time teachers can ask students to find and bring examples of the various aspects of writing they are learning to a class or group discussion. Simple tasks should be given so the reader is not distracted from enjoying reading. Ask for an example of a good description, a character that was appealing, an interesting beginning, or anything that has been explored during a writing workshop.

Handwriting

In the days of computers and the possibilities of new software taking over the role of handwriting, this section may seem irrelevant. Like many teachers, we are excited and challenged by the possibilities of technology but still believe that we have a responsibility to assist students in developing a fluent, legible handwriting style. The reasons for learning handwriting are linked to audience and purpose. There are certain times when handwriting the message is the most appropriate, such as with personal letters, notes, or cards. The learning styles of our students are also a consideration. Some may still prefer to plan and draft their writing with pen and paper while others may use more sophisticated means for these writing processes. When handwriting is utilized, having a fluent, legible style will enable the writer to write with maximum legibility and minimum effort.

Learning to form letters remains a component of literacy development and related to this is teaching good posture and pencil grip to reduce fatigue. Achieving this will involve short mini-lessons in order that correct letter formation is learned. Like spelling, handwriting is a tool for writing, and beautiful penmanship should never be the goal, although legibility is always important. The best time for students to practice what they learn in these lessons will be when they are doing purposeful writing, not exercises! However, for students having difficulties with handwriting, access to computers opens up the possibilities of being a successful writer.

Computer Skills

First and foremost students need to know about writing. Then they need to know how to use various forms of technology in all the stages of the writing process and when it is most appropriate. Many teachers are also providing regular access to keyboarding skills so students learn to touch type as early as possible. Posture and appropriate distance from the computer screen are also important aspects to be taught to students.

Students need:

- the skills of composing, cutting and pasting, and other features that support the revising process
- to know the possibilities that exist for publishing their writing in appropriate ways through using layout features, fonts, and other style features
- to know how to select appropriate graphics to accompany text
- to know about changing spacing and style when publishing
- to be familiar with software programs that will be useful to format a variety of texts

- to know what choices to make in order to present their writing appropriately for the audience and purpose.

Students need to be able to answer the question, "When will a computer-generated piece be more appropriate than a handwritten piece?" Often students (and their teachers) become distracted by some of the programs or features available. For example, the use of PowerPoint® is particularly popular in classrooms. While PowerPoint® offers an effective way of presenting certain information for certain audiences, it is not the only way. In some cases the actual skills involved in constructing a clever PowerPoint® presentation have become more important than the actual writing! The effective use of PowerPoint® or similar programs requires that students have carried out a great deal of research and written a draft that has been through careful revision. Once this is achieved students are ready to prepare appropriate electronic presentations by combining their computer skills of using graphics, sound, and animation with their writing skills. Students will have no trouble making appropriate choices in using technology to its potential once they understand both audience and purpose when writing.

A range of computer software and applications will have their place in the classroom, but the use will be determined by ongoing teacher assessment and evaluation. For example, if students are experiencing difficulty with get-ting started or organizing their writing, a program like Inspiration® may be useful. Jan does much of her thinking in "models" and produced numerous diagrams with Inspiration® while working on this book. When Michael in Grade 6 was asked why he used Inspiration®, he said: "I like Inspiration® because it is a way of putting everything in your head down onto a document." This tool has been an important factor in the development of Michael's writing.

The most important thing is to give students choices. We all think and work in different ways, so we need to ensure that when we model aspects of the process and the skills for writing we move outside our own preferences and show students what is possible.

Spelling

While many of the words we can spell we learn through reading, we also believe that spelling is a skill that needs to be taught. However, we strongly believe that the teaching and learning of spelling will be most successful within an effective, well-structured reading and writing classroom. We note that:

> Spelling develops as a consequence of engaging in the
> process of writing, and we would also assert that spelling

develops as a consequence of reading. In fact you must be
a reader in order to be a writer. This is not to say that one
precedes the other but, rather, that reading, writing and
spelling develop simultaneously and in transaction with
each other (Bean and Bouffler 1997, 11).

We see very little benefit in learning words for the sake of being able to
reproduce them in spelling bees or weekly written tests. Spelling is a part
of language and therefore the teaching of spelling must be consistent with
the teaching of reading and writing. While teachers often acknowledge this
relationship, it does not mean that this understanding is reflected in their
teaching of spelling. Far too often we see classrooms where exciting teaching
is happening in the areas of reading and writing but the teaching of spelling
is in isolation, usually from commercial textbooks, and totally out of context
with what is happening in the reading-writing lessons. When this happens
it is difficult for learners to make connections with what they are learning
about reading and writing. As students engage in learning to spell they need
to develop the understanding that spelling is a tool for writing. Thus, the
"sole purpose in teaching children to spell should be to enable them to write
clearly, confidently, and accurately" (Croft 1997, 1).

Any spelling program should include daily writing for a clearly articulated
audience and purpose—that is, an audience and purpose the student can
identify and relate to. Without such an audience and purpose the writer has
no reason to work on spelling and certainly has no reason to engage in the
revision of writing, editing and proofreading in particular:

What too often appears to be missing in planned spelling
instruction, especially as children move beyond their first
three years in school, is a continuous emphasis on "the
second 'R'"—writing—specifically writing for which
children have a personal interest and commitment. Such
writing supports learning to spell in some very specific
ways (Hughes and Searle 2000, 203).

DEVELOPING RISK-TAKING BEHAVIORS

Developing a community of learners depends on how the classroom
environment is established and the quality of the relationships. There is
often a certain culture across the whole school or building that defines it
as a place of learning. Some classrooms are exciting places to be, and those
are the places that children and adults love to work. An effective learning
environment can look very different in different classrooms. However, there

are certain features that we have noticed over many years in these engaging classrooms. In recent years there have been a number of research projects that describe what happens in these classrooms. Examples are Louden et al. (2005) and findings from projects conducted by Taylor, Pressley, and Pearson (2002).

Common features identified in these studies correspond with our observations. The research suggests these classrooms are places where students are:

- Actively engaged in appropriate, meaningful activities
- Engaged in reading, writing, listening, and talking daily
- Immersed in a classroom environment that is supportive of the learner and organized to scaffold learning
- Engaged in learning that responds to their needs based on ongoing assessment
- Guided to take some responsibility and make some learning decisions
- Guided by clear and appropriate explanations
- Given timely, focused, and explicit feedback
- Challenged through instruction that recognizes individual differences
- Learning in a welcoming, positive, and inviting classroom.

Appropriate shared goals, trust built from the knowledge that the students and teacher will support each others' efforts, and acceptance of differences are the three essentials of a class where all its members learn effectively and cooperatively. In a school with a positive climate, policies encourage and seek a cooperative, not a competitive, environment.

Cooperative structures create positive interdependence. This occurs when the members of a group understand that they cannot succeed unless the whole group succeeds. Goal interdependence occurs, for example, when a small group of children want to write and perform a play; the group has the same outcome or product in mind. Reward or recognition of interdependence can focus on the literacy product, such as a class book, a play, a newsletter, or a book discussion leading to a group mural. It may result in having the work displayed, shared with others, and receiving recognition from peers and the teacher. In Chapter 6 we talk about how to create a community of writers and risk-takers.

INSTRUCTION TO USE: KEY TEACHING STRATEGIES

The key teaching strategies of modeled, shared, guided, and independent writing are discussed in detail in Chapter 7.

Professional Development Activity: Reflecting on My Classroom Environment or Climate

The purpose of this professional development activity is to focus each teacher on his or her individual classroom environment or climate. We ask teachers to read a series of statements. They are then given time to discuss these statements in light of their views on their own classrooms. As an extension of this discussion, one person in the group acts as a scribe and notes key points on chart paper so these can be shared with the whole group as a point of closure.

Statement 1: Effective teachers seem to have high participation by their students in classroom activities. Their students pay attention, are engaged, and take great pleasure in learning.
Reflection: How do I know that students in my class are engaged in their learning?

Statement 2: In effective classrooms the environment is used as a teaching resource. The teaching is purposeful and students are always given an explicit understanding of the task. Explanations are clear and at an appropriate level. Lessons are designed to lead to substantial engagement. Modeling is well used and includes metacognitive explanations. Teachers in effective classrooms use and give the students a metalanguage to talk about and exemplify literacy concepts.
Reflection: Are the learning tasks in my classroom purposeful and appropriate to my learners? How effectively do I use language?

Statement 3: Effective classrooms are well structured and predictable. The teacher responds to learning opportunities and learning is paced appropriately. The teacher knows the students through effective assessment, and that information is used for planning and teaching. Learning is scaffolded through modeling and the classroom environment.
Reflection: How is my classroom structured to support all learners?

Statement 4: Differentiation is evident in effective classrooms. Teaching is structured around three or more groups and individual differences are recognized.
Reflection: How well do I differentiate instruction?

Statement 5: Effective classrooms are "nice" places to be. Good relationships are evident, and the classroom is a warm, welcoming place to be. There is a sense of equality, inclusivity, and awareness of the needs of others.
Reflection: What are the relationships like in my classroom? What are the indicators that my classroom is a happy, healthy learning environment?

Chapter 6: Helping Writers Consider Audience, Purpose, and Genre

In the model for teaching writing introduced in Chapter 5 (Figure 5.1), we suggested that the role of audience and purpose is critical in selecting certain genres when writing. We also suggested the important connections between audience and purpose to the process of writing and the skills required in engaging in that process.

There is an increasing awareness among teachers of providing audiences and purposes for writing to students and making these very explicit for them. The more the role of audience and purpose becomes evident, the more teachers come to understand what writing is and how it works (see Chapters 2 and 3). However, providing audiences and purposes for classroom writing is often interpreted as requiring something quite grand and time consuming for the teacher and students. While students can engage in projects that will take their writing far beyond the classroom, the truth is that a lot of the everyday writing we do should be valued and connections made to the audiences and purposes that exist. While this "small" writing may seem mundane, it is meaningful, it always has an audience and purpose, and it is where students may first learn about the role of audience and purpose in their writing. Remember that:

> Opportunities for writing occur throughout the entire school day. Not only should teachers provide time for children to write each day, but they should seize upon appropriate writing opportunities arising from every area of the curriculum. "Put it in writing," is the catch cry of one Year 3 class. "We write notes to our parents, letters to the Principal, to the canteen, the class next door. We write our thoughts after observations in Science or after listening to a piece of music. We write labels, captions, posters. There are

hundreds of situations which come up in a day which lend
themselves to all types of writing."

Each of these situations will have a different purpose for
writing, involving subjects and therefore "registers". In
Social Studies for instance, situations will arise when there
is a purpose for children to write reports, letters, diaries,
biographies, tables, time-lines, captions, posters, etc. (Butler
and Turbill 1984, 56).

These types of opportunities are still relevant to our classrooms, and we
must make the most of them.

Teachers who write themselves, we believe, are better teachers of writing
because they can get "inside" writing and understand the decisions a writer
must make in order to write in different genres. We encourage teachers to
write—to experience the process of writing—because they will be more
effective teachers of writing. As Butler and Turbill explain:

Teachers often read to, and with, their children; thus there
are regular demonstrations of reading behaviour for them
to use as models. This is not always true of writing. We
need to create opportunities which will allow children to
observe teachers writing. One teacher who does this said:
"I find that children are interested to see me putting ideas
together in writing. It is good to let them see me struggling
with sentences to get them right. Sometimes I ask children
to help me with the composition of certain things, such
as excursion notes, using the board I often write a few
sentences on my own at the start of writing sessions. Once,
when having trouble with a poem, I was surprised when
one of the boys offered me a collection of Spike Milligan
verses to use as models! The idea worked, and the children
were delighted" (1984, 54).

As well as writing in front of our students, we also need to think about
the purpose writing plays in our lives and share this knowledge with our
students. From our own stories we can help our students understand the
writing process and better understand the interplay between audience and
purpose and genres of writing as well as value the role that writing plays in
our every day lives.

Both of us are obviously writers. We take every opportunity when
working with children to share our experiences and tell our stories about the
writing, as Wendy describes in the following cameo.

Cameo: The Teacher as Writer

I tell my students about the writing I do for teachers and that I can spend months drafting and redrafting a chapter. I tell them about my treasured "green" book where I jot down my ideas as a resource, my spasmodic attempts at writing a picture book, and how these attempts remain hidden in files in my office. I tell them about the reports I write related to my job as well as my letters to family and friends (yes, I still write letters). I tell my students about the e-mails I write to friends and for business and how different they are, and I tell them about the notes I leave all over the house. I tell them the pleasure I get writing on cards for family and friends who are celebrating birthdays, anniversaries, and special occasions, and I tell them of the struggle I go through when I need to write a sympathy card or letter to a friend. I tell my students I have special paper for reports, note paper for messages, beautiful paper and cards for letters, airmail paper to write to my overseas friends, paper for the printer in a range of colors, and loads of scrap paper for printing drafts. All of my writing is connected with what I know about audience and purpose. My life is full of writing, some of it important and some of it not at all important in the eyes of others, but every single piece, hidden or heading out into the world, has an audience and a purpose.

Talking to students about our experiences in our day-to-day lives has the potential to make writing real for them, particularly those students who may not see reading and writing as a regular occurrence in their everyday lives.

In Chapter 7 we suggest some key strategies for teaching writing. The effective use of these strategies is dependent on the teacher's understanding of the writing process. We stress that modeled writing is one of the most powerful strategies available because of the "teacher talk." If planned and based upon their learners' needs, it is a powerful tool with which teachers can share not only their insights into the writing process but their enthusiasm as well.

We can all model writing, even if we do not see ourselves as writers, and we must keep the focus on audience and purpose. Everyone writes for audiences and purposes of some kind. If we feel our own experiences in writing are limited, we can share the thoughts of authors or even friends. For example, in the words of Fox and Wilkinson: "Please understand that good writing is something to aim for, not something to expect as soon as your pen touches the paper. If you anticipate that you won't be completely satisfied with your first draft you'll be less discouraged when you find that to be true" (1993, 24).

Students need to know even famous writers draft and redraft. Mem Fox's books for children are an excellent example of the impact of audience and purpose on writing. On her website and at various conferences she has shared interesting stories about her writing. Her recent book for children under five, *Where Is the Green Sheep?* has just 187 words. These few words took over a year to write. She is one author who talks about the agony of writing, but much of that agony comes from the search for the perfect words. This kind of revision would be impossible to comprehend if there was no understanding of audience and purpose.

EXAMINING CONNECTIONS BETWEEN AUDIENCE AND PURPOSE AND GENRE

As children learn to speak they come to understand the different audiences and purposes for their talk. Most children quickly learn that there are ways of saying things in order to achieve their purpose. They also come to learn that there are some places that certain talk is appropriate and others where it is not, that is, they quickly become aware of audience and purpose. We all have cute stories about when very young children get this wrong. However, by the time they are at school they usually have this worked out. We can help our students make this same connection to writing.

Genres can be oral or written. Some, such as a recount, are similar in structure and purpose in both the oral and written modes. Just as written genres have particular purposes and audiences so do oral genres. When teaching particular written genres, remember that many genres exist in spoken language as well as in written language. We should not underestimate the role of talking and listening in the writing classroom. Using the genres orally, naming them, and exploring their structures are parts of the writing process, particularly during the focusing phase (see figure 5.1).

SOME STRATEGIES FOR DEVELOPING TALKING SKILLS

Modeled Talking

Teachers talk most of the school day! Much of their talk becomes a model for the students to follow and use. If we want students to think about how to best achieve a particular purpose for a particular audience in an oral genre such as "requesting information," we can make explicit the thinking that we go through in order to structure our language use. For example, a teacher might say, "I want to know what time the train leaves, so I could say, 'Hey you, what time does the train leave?' Mmmm. Let me think. Is that the best way to achieve my purpose? Perhaps if I want to be sure to get the information I need I should be more polite and say, 'Excuse me please, what time does the train leave for Wollongong?' Yes, that sounds better."

During modeled writing teachers are using talk to think aloud how to be an effective writer. Teachers can also model how to use talk during and after writing. For instance, they might model the type of comments and questions writers ask about each others' writing.

Shared Talking

When engaging in shared talking, the teacher involves students in the process, often in whole class situations. Students might work in groups, talking and listening to each other and thinking aloud about the audience and purpose for the task in which they are engaged. For instance, organizing students to collaborate in pairs to write a science report will involve a great deal of shared talk as the students make decisions about how to best write their pieces.

Guided Talking

Guided talking is most commonly used during small group focus. The role of the teacher is to guide and respond to the students' needs in orally presenting a particular genre or during various phases of writing. During guided talking sessions, the teacher provides support to students to use spoken language for presenting ideas or information to a group of listeners in the form of a particular genre. The teacher works toward improving the students' skills in listening critically and responding to a variety of spoken texts. Guided talking may be used to support a group responding to a class assignment. It may be something simple, such as an oral presentation to the class to recap a study on a particular country. Alternatively, it may be guiding talk before or during the writing process in order to help a writer focus or refocus. After writing, the talk can be guided to provide audience feedback to the writing.

Independent Talking

During independent talking sessions, students apply the skills learned in modeled, shared, and guided talking sessions. What is important is for the teacher to provide appropriate opportunities for talking.

MOVING FROM ORAL TO WRITTEN GENRES

The relationship between audience, purpose and genre in our daily language use, be it oral or written, is one that we all have some knowledge about but we don't necessarily know that we know. As an example, consider the finals in the men's tennis at the U.S. Open. First let's imagine that we are sitting in the stands watching the match. One player is upset about a line call and is yelling at the umpire. We might turn to a friend and comment, "I think Jones' behavior is understandable. I would be angry, too." The purpose for the language is to share our thoughts—to give an opinion on what we see happening in front of us. The audience is a friend and the genre is simply a comment without much information because we both shared the experience.

However, if we are radio commentators for the same match, the audience now becomes interested tennis fans "out there." Then the purpose is to describe what is going on, since the audience cannot see what is happening. The language we use becomes descriptive, with some personal comment, such as, "Jones obviously believes that the ball was good. He has stopped playing and is now walking over to the umpire. This behavior is unacceptable, and the crowd is not impressed. Oh dear. Jones is now yelling at the umpire and pointing his racquet at him. I think if he could, Jones would hit the umpire with the racquet, he seems so angry."

Now if we were sitting on the sidelines in the press gallery as sports writers, we would be jotting down notes on our note pads or talking into a tape recorder. Some time after the event we would sit at our computers and reconstruct what went on using our earlier writing as a memory jogger. The audience is now people who read the sports pages of the newspaper. We don't know if they saw the match live or heard the radio broadcast, so our purpose is to provide enough information on the event so the readers know what went on. However, as we have had the opportunity to attend the media interview after the match, even though our language is now in the written mode and in the past tense, we can use the dialogue from the interview to bring authenticity to the writing. The language then might go something like: "Yesterday at Flushing Meadows the fans were provided with more entertainment than they had bargained for in the Men's Final between Jones and Spiros. In the third game of the fourth set, Jones became very upset with a bad line call. 'The umpire must have been asleep or otherwise he would have seen the ball was in,' Jones angrily reported at the media conference."

Each of these uses of language was about the same event, but because each had a different purpose and audience, the interplay between the two generated different linguistic choices. The resulting "texts," whether spoken or written, are significantly different from one another. It would have been senseless for us to have said to the friend what the sport writer wrote and vice versa.

TEACHING GENRES

The interplay among purpose, audience, and genre is what we need to help our students understand. Therefore teachers need to know the characteristics of the key genres that are most valued at the school and academic levels. The writing testing conducted by the National Center for Education Statistics (NCES) uses tasks that involve drafting, revising, and editing. Students are involved in writing narrative, informative, and persuasive texts. Each type of text has certain characteristics and makes different demands on the writer. For example:

> Narrative writing involves the production of stories or personal essays . . . . Sometimes narrative writing contributes to an awareness of the world as the writer creates, manipulates, and interprets reality . . . . Informative writing focuses primarily on the subject-matter element in communication. This type of writing is used to share knowledge and to convey messages, instructions, and ideas. . . . . Informative writing may also involve reporting on events or experiences, or analyzing concepts and relationships, including developing hypotheses and generalizations. . . . Persuasive writing emphasizes the reader. Its primary aim is to influence others to take some action or bring about change. . . . This type of writing involves a clear awareness of what arguments might most affect the audience being addressed (U.S. Department of Education 2001, 347).

Even though we might understand the different demands of writing certain genres, it is not uncommon that the writing experiences in classrooms tend to expose students to a narrow range of genres, in particular narrative and exposition.

The many genres that can be written and used orally tend to fall within the broad categories of literary and factual texts. Literary texts include narrative, literary recount, description, and review. Factual texts include factual description, information reports, procedural, factual recount, explanation, exposition, and discussion. All these genres have distinguishing features. We have developed a table, shown in Figure 6.1, of what we believe are the key school genres and their respective distinguishing features (see also Stephanie Harvey's list [1998, 167-189] and Mooney 2001).

Genre and Purpose	Distinguishing Structural Features (Text Level)	Distinguishing Grammatical Features (Word and Sentence Level)
Recount Used to document a series of events	Orientation: who, where, when. Events in chronological order Personal or evaluative comment	Action verbs to refer to events Nouns and pronouns Past tense Conjunctions and connectives Adverbs and adverbial phrases Adjectives
Narrative To entertain	Orientation Complication Resolution Coda	Metaphors, similes, and figurative language Consistent tense, usually past
Procedural To explain how to do something	Goal Materials needed Steps to accomplish goal	Action verbs Commands Precise vocabulary Adverbs; adverbial clauses Present tense
Factual texts such as reports Used to present information	General statement Description	General nouns Relating verbs Action verbs Timeless present tense Technical language Paragraphs, often with subheadings
Exposition Used to argue for or against a point of view	Statement of position Arguments Elaboration Restatement of position	General nouns Technical words Relating verbs Action verbs Thinking verbs Modal verbs and adverbs Connectives Evaluative language

Figure 6.1: Distinguishing features of key written genres

While these features are typical, all have the possibility to overlap and become blurred in the hands of sophisticated writers. For example, a narrative can contain factual description. In addition, all can be produced in a range of forms. For example, a narrative can take the form of a story, a ballad, a folktale, a myth, a legend, or a fable. A narrative has a structure that typically includes an orientation, a complication, and a resolution. However, any lover of narrative will know that while that is true much of the time, the exact structure may vary in certain texts. Take for example, the magnificent *Dear Children of the Earth* by Schim Schimmel. This is a narrative written in the form of a personal letter, beginning: "Dear Children of the Earth, I am writing this letter to ask for your help…" (1994).

Communicating with Students

Why are we exploring this and complicating the notion of genre? Simply to reinforce the reading-writing connection that was introduced in Chapter 2. Teachers must teach students about the range of genres, but at the same time help them to notice genres in use and be aware of the role of audience and purpose in shaping the various genres. It is through reading that students will see and learn what authors do.

When we talk to students engaged in writing various genres, some view the purpose for writing as being a "school" thing, and they perceive the audience only as the teacher. When students have this view, their writing tasks tend to become nothing more than classroom exercises. It can be difficult at times to find meaningful purposes and audiences for classroom writing, but the challenge can be met. The cameo later in this chapter provides examples of what one teacher has done to make audience and purpose a feature of her writers' workshop.

The same applies when reading with students. We find that students often can't identify the type of text or genre they are reading, and therefore they have no expectations of what they might find in the text in terms of language and text features. In other words, students often do not understand the connections between reading and writing.

How can students be successful in their writing, beyond writing to a formula, if they do not have an understanding of whom and what the writing is for? Are we teaching students to write beyond the classroom so they can select from the various genres they have learned in order to write in a way that achieves the required purpose for the specific audience? Experienced writers do this daily as they write notes, e-mails, memos, and newsletters and engage in various other types of writing.

A lack of focus on audience and purpose gives rise to comments that with the increased use of e-mail and other forms of quick electronic communication, spelling and punctuation will no longer be important.

Sometimes people writing electronic texts use a particular shorthand language and no punctuation. Writers of any age who understand the role of audience and purpose know that certain messages to certain people will need to be written in a particular way in order that the purpose is achieved. The audience must be acknowledged by the form the writing takes. This is to do with understanding the social, functional, and contextual nature of language. The same goes for text messaging on cell phones. In many instances we see this form of writing being used beyond the computer or cell phone. We have to help students see the role of audience and purpose and therefore when this form of writing will achieve its purpose and when it will not.

EXAMINING CONNECTIONS BETWEEN AUDIENCE AND PURPOSE AND THE WRITING PROCESS

Often the pressure to learn how to write various genres does not allow much time for the writer to fully engage in the process of writing. Students need time to move through the focusing and composing stages and then to engage in editing and proofreading in order to meet the demands of the intended audience and purpose. When process is absent, it is common to see writing that is mechanically correct but is simply not very good writing.

The following example comes from an eight year old who even with a potentially dull writing task seems to have grasped an idea of the purpose of writing. On the first day back at school after a vacation, many children must dread the topic, "My Holiday." Matthew's piece (Figure 6.2) was written in July (half way through the Australian school year) in Grade 2. It happened that he enjoyed his vacation and wanted to record his experiences. His writing is detailed and informative, and his audience is the teacher and himself. He seems to particularly enjoy personal writing. Although this writing is a first draft, its purpose and audience did not demand Matthew move this piece through the other phases of the writing process.

Other writing will move through all the phases of the writing process to publishing, but the audience and purpose of the writing will determine this. There would be no point, for example, for the piece from Matt's journal to be redrafted. The purpose for that writing was achieved in one draft. There are a range of ways of publishing writing depending on the audience and purpose:

> The reason for publishing is to make the writer's work available to potential readers. Publishing provides the motivation for children to correctly edit, rework, polish and finally proofread their pieces so they may communicate

their ideas clearly for others to read. Published work should be incorporated into the general reading resources used in the classroom. One effect of this is that children see their efforts are associated with the work of professional writers and are valued in their own right. Thus children come to perceive themselves as writers (Butler and Turbill 1984, 57).

My Holiday	Date 20·7·04

In the holidays on Sunday I went to Imax and saw a movie called Under The Sea. It was great. On Tuesday I went to soccer camp with James I did the same on Wednesday and Thursday. On the last day everyone played a game against the coaches. The score was two all. I was goaly and I saved a high kick. After the game everyone got a trophy and others got prizes. I had lots of fun at soccer camp. In the second week of the holidays on Tuesday I went fishing with my Dad. The second my bait hit the water a big snapper took it. It even knocked my fishing rod over. In the end my Dad had caught a lether jacket and a snapper. The next day I went fishing again and I didn't catch anything but my Dad caught a lether- jacket. It had a doctor in it. A doctor is a little animal with about 15 legs and it shares the food with the fish. We sometimes use them for bait. The next day I went fishing again. But we

didn't catch anything. Althogh I did hook something big. On Friday I chopped wood for about 2 hours. I did the same on Saturday and Sunday. On Monday a friend came over his name is Shawn.

What a terrific holiday Matt I hope you ate the fish you caught!

Figure 6.2: "My Holiday" by Matthew, age 8

Aside from small books, publishing may take the form of posters, labels, class or school newsletters, or letters. Software such as PowerPoint® provides another form of publishing. We come back again to audience and purpose for the writing in order to make good choices about appropriate forms of publishing. The notion of publishing for quality is key to the following description of approaches to publishing at Moonee Ponds West School:

> The upper primary children publish their polished
> pieces by neatly handwriting the text and adding simple
> illustrations. These are placed in a class library for all
> to read. However when a particularly good piece of
> writing is produced, the author is invited to publish it in
> a more sophisticated form. This may be as a "big book,"
> a well-illustrated picture book, or in any other form. In
> order to determine how the work will be presented, the
> young author, in consultation with the teacher, makes
> decisions about the size and shape of the book, the type of
> illustrations appropriate for the text, the style of lettering to
> be used, and the layout. Many standard picture books are
> consulted as models, and much discussion ensues about
> such matters as to whether to write in gold pen on black
> paper, whether to use collage or paint; whether to highlight
> particular words; indeed, whether to illustrate a page at all.
> The author chooses three or four helpers who will assist
> in making these decisions as well as doing some of the art
> work. The author continues to refine and polish the text.
> Sometimes, explicit details in the illustrations will mean
> the text can be modified. Similarly, the art work may need
> modification in the light of changes to the text. The quality
> of finished work is very high indeed.
>
> Marcia Saunders, a teacher at Moonee Ponds West,
> sees time spent on this publishing process as being
> worthwhile: "The children gain insights into the way in
> which professional writers work, and they see the richness
> that illustrations provide. . . . I am continually amazed at
> the effort they put into these books, and the quality they
> produce" (Butler and Turbill 1984, 57-58).

The beliefs underlying this teacher's actions include her commitment to the writing process, her understanding of audience and purpose, and the support given to students to work collaboratively. These same understandings can be applied to a range of forms of publishing related to different genres.

THE IMPACT OF AUDIENCE AND PURPOSE ON THE SKILLS OF WRITING

In a similar way to writing process, understanding audience and purpose for writing will impact on the skills we identified that are related to becoming a writer.

Spelling and Punctuation

In Chapter 5 we wrote about the importance of spelling and punctuation. However, there are times, depending on the audience and purpose, when spelling and punctuation are less important. This is related to understanding that language is contextual (see Chapter 1). There are certain contexts, or certain audiences and purposes for writing, in which spelling and punctuation are less important. Such writing would include a shopping list for oneself, a quick e-mail to a friend, a cell phone text message, or even a first draft for any piece of writing. A writer is not going to deliberately make spelling or punctuation errors, but rather knows instinctively that spelling and punctuation in these will be less important than in other writing.

Grammar

Audience and purpose determine choice of genre; therefore audience and purpose also determine the grammatical features or linguistic choices made to generate the particular text. Certain genres typically engage the writer in using certain grammar. A writer comes to learn through experience in reading, writing, talking, and listening that if writing an informational report, for example, common grammatical patterns will typically include such things as general nouns, relating verbs, timeless present tense, technical terms, and paragraphs. A narrative, on the other hand, will involve the use of adjectives and similes to create visual images, the use of time connectives, adverbs and adverbial phrases, past tense action verbs, and saying and thinking verbs. While there are no hard and fast rules, as young writers develop they become more aware of the grammatical features that are related to particular genres.

Handwriting and Computer Skills

Audience and purpose will determine the choice between handwriting and word processing and other computer-generated products. Some writing, such as cards, thank you notes, journal entries, note taking, and sometimes planning notes and first drafts will be more appropriately presented in handwritten form. When a computer-produced product is deemed to be most appropriate, the writer must make decisions related to layout, font, type size, use of headings and graphics, and so forth. Again, there are no fixed rules, and there will always be an element of personal choice, but there are times when it does matter. For example, if we were presenting a commissioned report on a project to a school district, it would be inappropriate for it to be submitted in handwritten form. There would be an expectation not only that such a piece of writing be produced using a word processor but also that it be presented in a certain genre and format. There will always be room for creativity, but again it is a matter of knowing the audience. These decisions can be discussed with students in order to help them see the way that writing is used beyond the classroom and the impact that audience and purpose plays from planning right through to forms of publishing.

In order to situate what we have shared above in the real world of teachers we present a cameo with two parts. The first part describes a teacher workshop. The second part describes how one teacher put what she learned at the workshop into practice in her classroom.

Cameo, Part 1: A Writing Workshop for Teachers

The workshop was organized for a group of four schools. The session began with a guided walk of the classrooms at the host school with a focus on beginning a dialogue about the teaching of writing. Visiting teachers were able to see classroom organization, the print environment created by the teachers and students, and examples of the everyday writing done in classrooms in addition to special writing projects.

The experiences that followed focused on:

- An exploration of "A Model for Teaching Writing" as a focus (see Figure 5.1)
- The teaching strategies of modeled, shared, guided, and independent writing
- The reading-writing connection and audience and purpose.

Teachers had the opportunity to explore how reading and writing are connected and flow together through approaching writing from a perspective of audience and purpose. The workshop concluded with some time to consider some of the thoughts of Shelley Harwayne on the teaching of writing. Her words inspire new ways to think about writing. She covers a range of ideas in her thoughts on "Reflecting on the Teaching of Writing," but the one that was particularly important to the teachers in the following cameo was related to school culture:

The school culture can either support or hinder the teaching of writing. It is easier to write and teach writing where there exists:

- a caring social tone
- a commitment to using time wisely
- authentic uses for student writing
- access to literature
- a deep respect for language
- a love of story
- a genuine curiosity about the world
- a passion for good writing
- a deep respect for childhood (Harwayne 2000, 47).

When these things come together they work toward developing a certain relationship between the teacher and the student and a certain culture in the classroom. As Part 2 of the cameo unfolds, we see what was possible in one classroom where these relationships were in place and a genuine learning culture was nurtured.

Cameo, Part 2: Visiting a Grade 4/5 Classroom

Three months after the workshop I was invited to visit one of the teachers. The class had two teachers working in a job share partnership. The children fondly refer to their teachers as Mrs. A and Mrs. B. Mrs. A had been inspired by some aspects of the teacher workshop she attended and had gone back to the classroom, already rich in approaches to teaching reading and writing, to try some of the new ideas.

The class is in a small school in the north of Sydney with a reputation of excellent teaching and learning. The principal and assistant principal are strong practitioners in the area of literacy and support a group of classroom teachers who also have a keen interest in this area. The result is consistency across the school that promotes enthusiastic young readers and writers. The standardized state test results reflect this enthusiasm, as does the quality of the everyday writing.

By invitation, I entered the 4/5 class (nine and ten year olds). Mrs. A told the students I loved to write and I had brought some of my writing in progress (this book in fact) to show the class. After I talked a little about my experiences with writing, Mrs. A asked the students to share and talk about some pieces they were proud of. Listening to some of the student pieces, I looked around the circle and was amazed to watch the students as their peers shared. Every child's face held a look of deep concentration and fascination. They listened with fierce intensity and applauded spontaneously when each reading was complete. I heard a range of genres in the children's writing. All the writing was engaging, and each student prefaced their reading

> with an explanation of how they came to write the piece they were sharing and the audience and purpose for the piece.
>
> After listening to several pieces I asked who liked writing. Every hand went up, with obvious enthusiasm. I asked how this was so. I explained that I often found some students keen on writing, but rarely a whole class.
>
> Some of the comments I heard were:
>
> "Writing is easier now because we have an audience for our writing."
>
> "Writing is easier because we have a choice."
>
> "Writing is easier. We got taught all the genres and that was a bit boring but then Mrs. A said we could have a choice and we could write to different audiences. Now it is more interesting than when our writing just stayed in our writing book. We write using lots of genres and have more fun. We also use technology more."

The changes Mrs. A and Mrs. B had made did not mean the students were not supported in their writing, as there were scaffolds around the room for each of the genres. Each student had a commercial book on writing that contained hints for writing and an explanation of each of the genres. They used it as a resource when they needed to check on structures and grammar related to a genre they were using. In addition, the students brainstormed things to write about. They had made a list of 1,094 topics that was proudly displayed on the wall for when "writer's block" might occur.

Dictionaries were available, and there were six computers in the back of the room. It seemed that Mrs. A and Mrs. B gave the students everything they needed to be writers, including an understanding that writers must first and foremost consider who they are writing for and what the purpose of that writing will be. What has resulted is remarkable.

For the eleven-week term, Mrs. A and Mrs. B had asked the students to keep a record of their writing, including the audience and purpose for each piece. This is a form of ongoing assessment for the teachers and also a form of self-assessment and monitoring for the students. The aim is to make the students more aware of what they are writing and for them to monitor the genres they are using to ensure there is some variety in audience and purposes in their writing. Selecting the following writing samples was extremely hard, as every piece was worthy of inclusion.

Example 1: Joyce's Audience and Purpose Record

Joyce is a Korean student who has been in Australia and at this school for two years. She has made remarkable progress with English under the guidance of these wonderful teachers. Joyce's piece, with her own spelling, appears in Figure 6.3. Joyce has a sense of audience, but her main purpose is to demonstrate her learning of English.

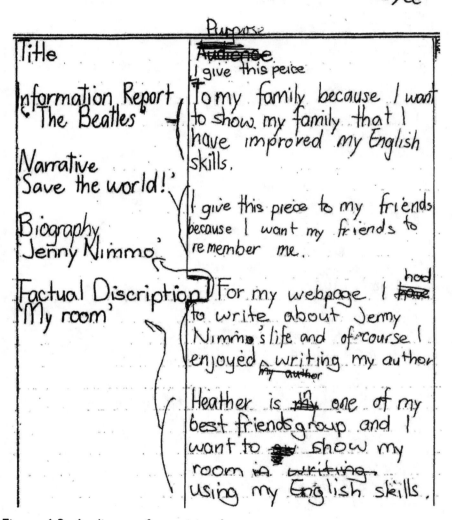

Figure 6.3: Audiences for writing: Joyce

Example 2: Peter's Grasp of Audience

Peter is also a Korean student and has been in Australia for one year. The sample in Figure 6.4 shows the first page of his record of writing. His grasp of audience is very practical.

text type 1 done

Title: Nick's escape.
Perpise: Make him happy.
Audance: Nick.

Title: Egypt
Perpise: Give him birthday present and make him special
Audance: uncle ikon.

Title: Who am I?
perpise: he like to Guess
Audance: Grand pa

Title: why we keep our body clean?
Perpise: my brother doesn't like to do shower.
Audance: brother

Title: water Hole
Perpise: My mum like to read
Audance: mum

Title: cricket
Perpise: to he want a learn about cricket
Audance: cousin John

Title: My bed room.
Perpise: tell every one what is my bed room looks like
Audance: Mrs walmsley

Title: biography
perpise: tell about his life
Audance: Mitchell

Figure 6.4: Audiences for writing: Peter

Example 3: Claire's Personal Reflections

Claire's list in Figure 6.5 shows the writing she has completed. Also included is her personal reflection. The reflection was done at the request of the teachers as a form of assessment. The task was for students to reflect on themselves as writers. The comments are interesting and informative for these teachers as they begin to think about planning for a new class of students. Research (see Chapter 3) acknowledges the role of an effective teacher in student learning. One of the markers of an effective teacher is the relationship that develops between teacher and student. The comment that this teacher is "pushing me to the limits (in a nice way)" is an important indicator of the successful relationships in this classroom.

Claire.

TITLE	PURPOSE	AUDIENCE
Nutcracker	to show people my love of this story and its ballet	Friends who don' understand the special ballet styl
Leonardo Da Vinci	He sets an example of creating new things	Anneke, she loves inventions
How to make Jordan Brink	to say sorry to Jordan for getting her in trouble.	Jordan Brink an example leader.
Miniature Donkeys	Just for the love of a cute animal.	Animal lovers in my friendship group.
Big Boy	I wanted to show how much I love my family	Heather, she knows my fami so much and Max always makes her laugh

| MY EXPERIENCE AS A WRITER |

I have to admit at first I didn't like writing at all, it didn't suit me, and I couldn't really do it. But then I had Mrs A as a teacher and by pushing me to the limits (in a nice way) I made it I wasn't the best at it and I had written less then a few people but I did it and my experience and perspective on writing changed.

Figure 6.5: Audiences for writing plus reflection: Claire

Example 4: Olivia's Persuasive Writing

Olivia's writing for the term shown in Figure 6.6 shows a good range of purposes and consequently genres. Her review of Duckmaloi, a property rented by her family for a weekend, appears in Figure 6.7. After completing this piece of persuasive writing Olivia e-mailed it to the owner of the property. The owner responded and asked if she could use the first paragraph in her new tourism brochure! There have been several successes in getting published beyond this classroom that have added to the enthusiasm for writing.

Olivia		
Title	~~Pup~~ Purpose	Audience
Retell: The Good Samaritan.	To welcome the Bishop to O.L.P.s	Bishop David Walker
Dear Bishop David	To Explain TGS	"
Review, Trixie Belden The Secret of The Mansion	To put on web page and let people read Trixie Belden books	The people who read it
Review, Duckmaloi Park.	To introduce Duckmaloi park to other families	Jane (owner)
Biography, Julie Campbell	To talk about Julie Campbell	The people who read my web page
Explanation, Christmas Day/ Newletter	To announce the Christmas day to the school	The school
Procedure, How to dowload digital camera photos etc etc	To teach dad how to use the camera.	Dad
Recount, Basket ball Gala Day (with Audrey)	To tell the school about the gala day instruct	The school (Newletter
Explanation, Talent show	To ~~tell~~ the teacher to pick 2 dances for the show	Teachers

Figure 6.6: Audiences for writing: Olivia

Duckmaloi Park!

Parents are you looking for an ideal place in the countryside to get away from everything?
Why not try Duckmaloi Park!

Duckmaloi Park is a comfortable 7 bedroom house with 15 beds. With its barbeque area, spacious deck, amazing views and double fire place you will surely go back for a second visit!

Duckmaloi Park is a ten minute drive from Oberon. There is LOADS of entertainment. In Oberon you can participate in activities like visiting the Jenolan Caves, they are exquisite! You can also go horse riding OR visit the Wangara Falls, there is stacks to do! At Duckmaloi Park you can go out into the massive backyard and like me play golf. Or even better you can go 4 wheel driving to the creek or find a spot to light a bonfire. Something extra fun we did was tie the go-cart to the car and ride around on the dirt road! Either way you will have heaps of fun!!!

The kitchen is fully equipped with the general facilities for your use, cook top, double electric oven, cutlery, cooking utensils, electric beater, fridge, microwave and dishwasher but with the barbeque you can cook many yummy things like bacon and eggs, sausage sandwiches, pancakes or fish!

The lounge room has a guarantee that you will find comfy seating near its second warm fireplace. There is also a stereo, TV and DVD for you to watch if you wanted to veg out! Through the lounge there are some glass, french doors that lead you outside onto the deck where you can take in the breath taking views of the Duckmaloi Valley.

Duckmaloi Park is a farm so it has plenty of space to have fun on! If you go 4 wheel driving you have a 100 % chance of coming across some animals. I saw kangaroos, cattle and blue tongue lizards!

I LOVED Duckmaloi Park and having the opportunity to go down to the river and go Go carting! (Though having a fall wasn't so great!) I would recommend it to a group of families of all ages and sizes. It is fabulous with its warmth and drama free feeling!

© Olivia Rorke
4/5 student
OLPS Primary School
West Pymble

Figure 6.7: Review of Duckmaloi Park by Olivia

Example 5: Heather

Teachers often express concern over writing that is so poor that it is difficult to conference with the student. Sometimes they don't know where to start to support the student. This challenge occurs when students don't understand the idea of audience and purpose. They just write, and sometimes their main focus is on the wildest topic they can think of. The writing goes on and on and lacks structure. These students often come to perceive themselves as poor writers. Heather was one such writer. One way teachers can support students like Heather is described below.

Mrs. A read aloud the description of the barn in *Charlotte's Web* by E. B. White (see Chapter 1). She asked the students to listen carefully to the language used to describe the sights, sounds, and smells of the barn. The task that followed was simply for the students to write a description of the place where they sleep. The focus was on description and the purpose was to describe this place for others in the group. As a follow up, students were asked to share other descriptions that they discovered in their personal reading. This is another example of the reading-writing connection. Heather's piece in Figure 6.8 is a description of her bedroom and is one example of the writing emerging from this simple workshop.

Example 6: A Poem by Anneke

Mrs. B. instigated the writing below when she suggested that the children could write something special for Mrs. A's birthday. This piece stood out because of its form, humor, and honesty. Anneke explained that her purpose was to give a gift to her teacher, and she worked independently on the poem. The final piece, shown in Figure 6.9, was typed on the computer and printed with a small flower motif at the bottom of the page. It is an insightful piece of writing in terms of what Anneke perceived about her teacher. She also had a little fun with the mention of spelling tests, as tests are not common practice in this classroom.

My Bedroom

My Bedroom

When you enter my room it takes a while to get used to it but eventually you'll fall in love with it. The thing I love most about my room is I know all of my possessions are mine to keep and no one can take them away from me.

Stuck on my door is a prayer for my family, it even includes my pet dog Oscar. I have to admit my wardrobe is really big, enormous is a better word for it. Inside my wardrobe are my clothes and sometimes it might surprise you what you find in there. To the left is my warm, comfortable, inviting bed. Lying on my bed are all of my 24 treasured sweet, cuddly soft animal toys. Beside my bed is my bedside table where I keep all my half finished books and in the centre of the pile lies my glowing lamp, which I read tales about magic and wonder under.

My bookshelf is where all of the magic comes from. I don't exactly keep all my books tidy but I always manage to find the book I'm looking for. Opposite my bed is my window where my curtains drape across it giving my room a mysterious feel. Under the window is a box where I keep all my old childish toys but I could never get rid of them. Next to my childish toys is my shoe rack. I have my horse slippers, runners, my good shoes and in the corner my evil school shoes.

In the middle of the ceiling is my light hanging down .My light is my blazing sun that no dark corners can escape. When you turn it on its light sparkles on the ceiling and fills up the entire room but when you turn it off, my room seems a lonely and sad waist land. On happy, off sad. But as long as I have my room with me that light will keep burning bright.

By Heather Oesterheld.

Heather you have done a beautiful job with this description. It feels as if your room is alive. There are some fabulous descriptive sentences.

Figure 6.8 Description by Heather

Dear Mrs A,

When you walk in the room it makes our hearts yearn
With a teacher like you it's easy to learn

You're kind and patient, you're always full of joy
It's no difference to you if we are a girl or a boy

You're great with music and have a beautiful voice
When it comes to songs you make the right choice

You're very creative and full of ideas
The fabulous show was the best in years

You specialise in English and teach us to spell
Even though in spelling tests we feel quite unwell

You're enthusiasm and love has helped me to grow
You're an amazing teacher who I'm proud to know!

Happy Birthday to wonderful teacher!

Love Anneke

Figure 6.9: Anneke's poem for her teacher

Example 7: A Novel by Katie

This last example, shown in Figure 6.10, is the first page of a novel by Katie. She would like to be a writer like her aunty. Katie included a dedication on the first page that went as follows:

For my family, who have always loved, cared for and encouraged me to do my best.
For my friends at OLPS, I do hope you enjoy reading my story.
For my teachers Mrs A. and Mrs B., who helped me put my first novel together, I couldn't have done it without them.

City Life by Katie Gould

Published OLPS Primary School

2004

Once upon a time there was a girl named Jade who lived on a farm with her horse, Midnight and her dog, Buster. She lived with her mum, dad and her 16 year-old brother. She loved her home and her age (11) and most of her family. Her mother always wished they lived in a mansion in the big city like she did when she was young. The only problem was that they didn't have enough money. Jade didn't want to see her mother upset so she decided to cheer her up. She loved her home so she decided she would do something that would be unlikely to make money out of. And then she had it. She would get her mother a lottery ticket. Then she would tell her mother to cheer her up.

She grabbed fifteen dollars from her wallet and ran down the stairs. She was half way out the door when Ben called out, "Where are you going?" She froze; that was a good question. How was she going to get to town on foot? It was 6 miles away and you're not allowed to drive when you are 11 but then again, you are when you are 16. She looked over at Ben thoughtfully. Ben looked suspiciously back.

"I need a lift to town," she said trying to look honest.

"Why?" he replied.

"Oh no" Jade thought to herself, "now what will I say?"

"Well?" he asked.

"Um..." she began.

Figure 6.10: A novel by Katie

The writing emerging from this class is due not only to the approaches of these two teachers, but to the emphasis placed on writing beginning in the first year of school for these students. Throughout the school there is a wonderful culture of valuing reading and writing. Learning is certainly made easier when students can move from one class to the next and have their knowledge built upon rather than experience a new approach each school year. We have found that once teachers have a deep understanding of the connections between reading and writing coupled with an understanding of the interplay among audience, purpose, and genre there is no stopping the many innovative practices that they begin to implement. These in turn both excite and enhance the teaching of writing and begin to produce young writers who not only perceive themselves as writers but enjoy writing and want to keep doing it!

There are many ways to get students to begin their writing by thinking about audience and purpose. The activity below is an effective way to work with students who may not be making this connection.

If you have not already done so, give your students some opportunities to work collaboratively in groups. Talk about the skills they will need to work this way, particularly active talking and listening. Group the students according to their independent reading level. Each group will need four or five pieces of reading material at their independent reading level:

1. A small article from a magazine or newspaper appropriate in content
2. A short poem
3. A letter
4. A persuasive text—perhaps an extract from a travel brochure.

Group leaders guide their group through the following questions, applying them to each of the pieces:

- Who might have written this?
- Why was it written?
- Who was it written for?
- Was it successful for the purpose and audience for whom it was written?
  An elected leader from each group reports back to the whole class.
  Each group is encouraged to discuss their decisions.

Finish the workshop by asking the students to get their writing folders and, in small groups or pairs, apply the same questions to their own writing.

Chapter 7: The Four Pillars for Managing Writing Instruction

The past chapters have been about the "why" of teaching writing, and we have spent many pages sharing what we believe is the "what" of teaching writing. This chapter is about the "how." We would love to be able to say, Okay—here it is. This is how you do it!

1. Take 24+ children
2. Take 24 pieces of paper and 24 pencils
3. Mix the two together and let them loose.
4. After 20 minutes all 24 children will produce perfect pieces of writing.

However, having read the previous chapters, you know that there is no one way to teach writing, and there is no one way to organize for the teaching of writing. There are, however, some important factors to take into account when organizing ourselves and our students for writing. These we have called the *Four Pillars for Managing Writing Instruction*. They are:

- Time and timing
- Resources
- Teaching strategies
- Assessment.

Each of these factors is contingent upon the other and in no way can be mutually exclusive. However, we talk about each in broad terms and share actual classroom examples throughout this chapter. Some of what we say in this chapter may repeat what we have said elsewhere. We don't apologize for this because our beliefs, practices, and how we put them into play are so interconnected (or should be).

PILLAR 1: TIME AND TIMING

The first pillar is time and timing. Writing needs time. Donald Murray tells us that this time needs to be regular and predictable, what he calls the "writing habit" (1982, 43). He cites many professional writers who talk about having to discipline themselves to sit and write for at least two hours daily. These writers agree: writers write. So what does this mean for our classrooms? It means that every day we need to provide adequate time for students to practice the processes of writing. This means not only time to put pencil to paper or fingers to keyboard. It means time to talk, time to think, and time to share. It also means time to read and be read to.

Equally as important is the timing of the writing time. Trying to find predictable, quality time daily is a challenge given the busy schedules many schools have. Many teachers do, however, make quality time for writing each day. One teacher, Miss M, begins the day with her kindergarten students by modeling a daily message, or news. This might be as simple as "K2 is going to swimming today." This teacher modeling is followed by the children going to their desks and writing or drawing their news for that day in their News Book. Each piece is dated, and the teacher makes time to meet with at least one group of children a day to listen to their news. After five or so minutes of writing, the children share what they have been working on with their partner. All this takes around fifteen minutes daily. As the year progresses the children are encouraged to write more than draw, using temporary spelling and copying words from the many word charts around the room. This time eventually becomes writers' workshop in her classroom.

Mr. G, a Grade 5 teacher, has a set time of 40 to 45 minutes three times a week for writers' workshop. However, he also has a daily time for what he calls "Power Writing," an idea that he adapted from Macrorie's "Free Writing" (1985). This is scheduled straight after sustained silent reading in the morning session. At the beginning of the year, he gives his students a book they label "Power Writing." Mr. G explains that while there will be other times in the week when they will be writing, this time is for them to "free write." He draws the analogy that to be an effective sports person (both the girls and boys are keen soccer players) they have to practice their skills and develop their fitness and muscles so they have power as players. So it is with writing, he explains. The purpose of the power writing time is to develop their writing "fitness and power" for an audience of self.

The students brainstorm all the topics they can think of to write about. These are written on small strips of paper and put into a container called the "Topics Jar." Each morning a student chooses a topic from the jar and reads it to the class, who are all sitting ready with pencil in hand. "Begin," says Mr. G, and he turns on the timer for five minutes (initially the timer was for three minutes). All students must write on the chosen topic. If they can't think of something to write they must write "blah blah" until their next thought comes. When the timer buzzes they stop and read over their writing. No one else reads their writing; no one corrects it. However, they do turn to their writing partner and either read the writing or parts of it or talk about it. Over the year they discuss aspects such as ideas that appeared in the writing that surprised them, interesting phrases or vocabulary that they know came from something they read or heard read to them, and many other aspects of the process of writing. All this takes no more than ten to twelve minutes, but it is a productive use of time for writing. Often the children take one of the pieces of writing begun during power writing and continue to draft and revise it during writers' workshop later in the day.

Integration ↕ Explicit and Systematic Teaching ↕ Assessment for Reporting ↑ Assessment for Teaching				
	Whole Class Teaching	Modeled Reading	Modeled Writing • Handwriting • Spelling • Grammar • Structure	Modeled Talking and Listening • Grammar • Structure
		Shared Reading • Spelling • Grammar • Structure	Shared Writing • Grammar • Spelling • Punctuation • Structure	Shared Talking and Listening • Structure • Grammar
	Small Group Teaching	Small Group Instructional Reading • Guided Reading • Reciprocal Teaching • Reader's Circle • Literature Circles	Guided Writing • Spelling • Punctuation • Grammar • Structure	Guided Talking and Listening • Grammar • Structure
	Independent Learning	Independent Reading • For a variety of purposes	Independent Writing • For a variety of audiences and purposes	Independent Talking and Listening • For a variety of audiences and purposes

Figure 7.1: An overview of a literacy block

Writers' workshop is typically scheduled for approximately one hour of the literacy block time. This block of time will vary according to age group, school organization, and the personal preferences of the teacher. Figure 7.1 shows the numerous aspects that need to be considered when developing a literacy block and the place of writing in that block of teaching time. Not only is it important for the teacher to consider the balance of reading, writing, and listening and talking, but also a balance among whole class, group, and individual learning opportunities. The model also highlights the connection between teaching and assessment.

This model can serve as a reminder of the considerations in planning and organizing for literacy. The teacher's role is to plan a balance of the key teaching strategies in order to meet the needs of the students. Some of the skills of reading, writing, and listening and talking can be taught through the key strategies. For example, spelling can be taught during a modeled writing session.

Figure 7.2 is an example of the literacy block action in a Grade 3 classroom.

Time Spent in Minutes (120 minutes total)	Class Organization	Activity
10	Whole class	Modeled reading
30	Groups	Guided reading group with teacher • Other groups doing various reading, writing, and listening and talking activities • These activities will provide opportunities for students to practice what they have been learning
15	Whole class	Sharing what they learned in their groups
10	Individual	Sustained silent reading
10	Whole class	Modeled or shared writing
30	Groups and individual	Guided writing group with teacher, others writing independently
20	Whole class	Sharing of writing

Figure 7.2: How Miss M organizes her literacy block

PILLAR 2: RESOURCES

Our second pillar is the resources available for the teaching of writing. This pillar includes materials and human resources as well as how to organize everything to best suit the learning environment.

The Classroom Environment

Creating an environment where students can learn and engage in the writing process is an important consideration. Learning becomes extremely laborious if the learner is not a participant in the process. Students need the time to experiment with writing regularly and practice what they are learning. Therefore, the teacher's role in supporting and scaffolding the learner is crucial. Central to achieving this is creating an environment where the students are safe to take risks and "have a go."

The environment the teacher creates must be one where students want to write and feel comfortable exploring written language. Writing development needs encouragement and support based on focused observation that results in teaching which meets the needs of all students.

The classroom environment is important. It needs to be attractive but more importantly reflective of what the students are learning. Materials must be accessible to the students and displayed where they can easily be referred to and used. This provides a challenge for most teachers who find themselves in classrooms with limited available space for displays at a level where the students have easy access. Creativity is the key. Teachers should watch how these materials are being used, and if access appears to be restricting their use, move them.

In the early years, the basic resources should include the alphabet, the days of the week, and the months of the year displayed in a prominent place. There is nothing more frustrating for a young writer than spending the bulk of independent writing time struggling to "sound out" the day of the week as they attempt to begin their piece by writing the date. Teacher modeling before the writing workshop and guided print walks to read the words and charts around the room will help students as readers and remind them where the words are if they need them in their writing. Every classroom needs to have a range of reading materials, including children's literature (fiction and nonfiction), poetry, magazines, pamphlets, and other community texts. These materials should be freely available for the students to read, use as models, and check spelling. Reference materials such as dictionaries, thesauruses, and atlases are also necessary.

The following items are useful on the desk for beginning writers:

- their name printed clearly
- an alphabet card or strip (if the strip is presented in a single horizontal line it is simple for the child to run their finger across the letters to find the one they are looking for)
- a word bank of commonly used words
- a have-a-go book (see example in Appendix 8).

In many classrooms students write their drafts in blank books; others use sheets of paper. If using the latter it is important to have appropriate storage for the paper so the drafts don't become lost or end up in the trash. For some students the use of writing folders can be supportive. Students can date work and store it in a way that aids the monitoring of progress by both the student and the teacher. This will assist in evaluating growth in writing and spelling. Other support materials for individual children may be stored in their personal writing folder when the teacher considers them appropriate. These may include writing guides, personal word lists, and lists of things to do, such as how to get started.

Access to computers in classrooms varies. While this access will continue to increase, it is presently rare that children compose directly into a word processor. The computer is more often used for developing the final product.

Human Resources

Many teachers organize to have support during the writing time. For some, the additional support may be the ESL teacher or reading specialist; for others it may be volunteers. Having extra adults to help with spelling, listening to the writing, assisting in the editing, or publishing the writing on computers is a bonus in the writing workshop period. We know of schools where volunteers are called for at the beginning of each year and many family and community members usually step forward. Another school organizes with the local university for student teachers to come into the rooms. The school runs a short course for the students to provide them with the school policy on writing. Students are then asked to allocate at least one hour at the same time each week. Another school principal seeks volunteers from the senior citizens' group at the local church at the beginning of each school year. The principal holds short meetings to describe how volunteers can support the teacher as well as discussing the ethics of working with children. Such support can be worthwhile, but we caution that it is the role of the school to make sure that volunteers are made cognizant of appropriate behavior regarding children. Volunteers are always an invaluable support but should never take on the same role as the teacher.

Arrangement of Desks

The physical arrangement of the room is important. Desks arranged in groups encourage sharing and peer cooperation. The decision on arrangement of desks will depend on the ability of the class (or group of children) to be able to work collaboratively and at times independently. It may also useful to provide one or two quiet, private areas. While learning is a social activity, there are times when some students need to be uninterrupted. Some teachers like to set up a writing corner where students can go during the day when they write.

Adjusting to the Needs of Individual Students

Individual students in any class will have different needs. It is important that students can move around the room to gather resources and discuss their writing and spelling, but for some they will work more efficiently in a quiet classroom. Even at an early age children can discuss the problem of classroom organization and suggest routines that will suit everyone. One suggestion is that writing begins with a silent writing time. This time allocation may begin as short as two minutes in kindergarten and be as long as twenty minutes with older children. This allocated time gives everyone the opportunity to mentally prepare for the task before them, locate their work, and begin writing. It will also give the teacher an opportunity to do a little writing that can be shared. This way the teacher can truly become a member of the group. Alternatively, it might provide a time for some one-on-one conferencing to help students' progress with the writing.

PILLAR 3: TEACHING STRATEGIES

The third pillar comprises the many teaching strategies that teachers use. We suggest that there are four broad teaching strategies for writing that allow the teaching to move from teacher directed and teacher controlled to learner directed and learner controlled.

Strategy for Teaching	Teachers' Role	Students' Role
Modeled Writing	Teacher directed and controlled Teacher holds the pen	Students observe and listen
Shared Writing	Teacher directed, with shared control between teacher and students Teacher holds the pen and at times invites students to take the pen	Students given opportunities to interact; make choices
Guided Writing	Direction originates from students' needs Teacher facilitates and scaffolds student(s)	Student given opportunity to take control and to interact; make decisions with guidance from teacher Student holds the pen
Independent Writing	Teacher provides opportunities for students to write	Students are responsible for their writing and are working independently Student holds the pen

Figure 7.3: From teacher to student-directed and controlled strategies

Modeled Writing

The teacher provides a model of a proficient writer in progress and "thinks aloud" about the writing process as the modeling takes place. Students are the observers of the writing process in action. The teacher plans to model any aspect of the writing process or related skills depending on needs. Modeled writing should take place daily in the early years and remain an important strategy even when students become more proficient. The key is that the lesson is short and very focused, and the teacher is cognizant of the language used. The *teacher talk* should be about the focus of the lesson, not management language. Teaching points should be planned ahead and be in response to the needs of the students. Modeled writing can be a whole class lesson, but at times teachers may work with a small group in order to extend or support them.

A modeled writing lesson for beginning writers might sound something like this, as the teacher talks aloud while writing in front of the class or group:

"I am going to write a journal entry this morning. I think I will write about something I did last night. Now, let's get started. I know I have to start my writing over here (teacher marks starting point), and I remember that I must start with a capital letter." The teacher writes "I."

"One thing I will remember to do today is to leave a space between my words so it will be easy for you to read."

The teacher writes: "I went to the" and reads as she writes. "'I went to the …' Now I want to write 'movies' and I know that 'movies' starts with 'm.' I also know the word is on our word wall."

The teacher looks at the word wall and asks one of the students to find the word. She writes "movies."

"Now I am going to go back and read this sentence to make sure it makes sense. ' I went to the movies…' Mmm, I think I will keep going and tell you when I went to the movies." The teacher writes "last," saying the word slowly as she writes. She says "night" and then says, "I know I have seen this word before, and it is one I can't sound out. I am going to copy that word."

The teacher picks up *Night Noises* by Mem Fox, locates the word she wants on the front cover, and writes the word on the board.

The teacher might continue in this way if she is modeling using strategies to try writing a word, or alternatively if the teacher wants to model expanding the writing she might read the text and say: "I haven't written very much and am a bit stuck. Who could ask me a question about what I have written?"

The teacher would listen and would talk in response to one or two questions.

"Thank you for those questions. I have some good ideas now. I am going to write about who I went with, and I think I will write a bit about what I saw. There are lots of things I can write to make my writing more interesting."

The lesson would continue for about ten minutes. The focus of this lesson is learning to use capitals and to write a simple sentence with spaces between the words. Further, the purpose is to model for the students where to find words in the room. Toward the end the lesson the focus moves to expanding the text. With older students the same process would apply and the lesson could be slightly longer. The focus might be on the structure of a particular genre or a particular aspect of spelling, punctuation, or grammar. Whatever the focus, it should be in response to observed needs of the students.

Modeled writing is a "think aloud" demonstration of the writing process. All genres can be modeled, including narratives, reports, expositions, short answers to a test, note taking, instructions, and outlines. Any stage of the writing process can be modeled: focusing or planning, drafting, editing, re-writing, proofreading, layout, or publishing. And any use for writing can be modeled: writing to communicate, writing to think, or writing to learn. The role of audience and purpose can be explicitly demonstrated during modeled writing.

As shown in the example above, in a modeled writing demonstration the teacher typically creates text in front of a group of students explaining *why* they are doing *what* they are doing *as* they are doing it. Teachers write on chart paper, a transparency on an overhead projector, the chalkboard, a whiteboard, or an interactive whiteboard while the students listen and watch.

The many purposes of modeled writing include:

- Demonstrating the process of writing: drafting, editing, proofreading, re-writing, and publishing
- Demonstrating the process of writing a particular genre, focusing on the features of that genre, the purpose, and the audience
- Demonstrating the spelling system of language
- Demonstrating the grammar system of the language
- Demonstrating the punctuation system of the language
- Letting novice writers in "on the secret" of what is usually a silent activity.

Teachers need to choose one or two main purposes for each modeled writing lesson and not overload the students with too much at once.

When to use modeled writing and what to model

Modeled writing is an ideal way to introduce students to the writing process itself, to refinements in the process, or to a new genre. It can occur in a whole class or in a small group depending on the needs of the students. The obvious advantage of a small group is that it is efficient and far easier to engage all students, meeting individual needs, although this kind of grouping tends to be more in line with guided writing.

Modeled writing should happen regularly. The more often students observe an expert in action during different stages of the process, the more chance they have of learning that which we want them to learn. It can be used in all content areas, not just during the writing workshop. The best time to demonstrate how to write a genre such as a science report, for instance, is in the time allocated to teaching science.

The stages in the writing process: Teachers need to model the stages in the writing process. As we have previously said, writing is a process. It is not something that happens miraculously by gifted people called authors. The finished product does not fall off the pen in one neat, perfectly composed, perfectly spelled, perfectly penned state. It is a messy and often protracted activity.

Typically, the writing process falls into three main phases: before writing, during writing, and after writing. Writers get ready to write, draft write, revise, edit, proofread, go public, and/or publish, seek a response from a reader, and experience some change in their attitude to themselves as writers. This description of the writing process appears linear, but in reality it is recursive. Everybody creates their own version of this process every time they write. But, in general, they go through these phases in some form or other.

Identifying audience and purpose: It is essential to identify the audience and purpose of the writing because that determines everything a writer does throughout the entire process. It determines the genre, the linguistic choices, the tone, the necessity for adhering to conventional spelling and grammar, and so on.

For example, the teacher might say:

- This is a report for my term paper. It had better be good because Mrs. Jager is not that impressed with my work this term.
- This piece is a story for the children in first grade. That means I will have to write a draft first, edit it, then try it out on some young childrren. so this first draft can be pretty messy since I'm the only one who's going to read it at the moment.
- Mmmm, what should I write about? I know! "A Dog Called Miffy." All little kids are interested in dogs.
- Now, what's a good lead? That's always hard to think of straight away so I think I'll just start writing.

Defining the exact focus of the task: If the writing is a report or an essay that has been set, the first thing to model is how to define the task. This includes identifying the meaning of the set question. Show how key words in the question or instruction signal or reveal the exact focus required. For example:

- "Compare and contrast" means that I have to look at the similarities *and* differences, not just the similarities, like in that earlier question that said "Compare . . ."
- "Referencing at least three sources," means I have to look up and cite at least three different books. I already have one so I'd better go to the library to get a couple more.
- "Explain the life cycle of a caterpillar with diagrams" means I have to include both a diagram and some writing. They probably want captions, too. I'd better make sure one of those books has something to help me do that.

Deciding the subject and theme: The whole process of writing is easier if writers distinguish between two concepts—subject and theme. The subject is what they are writing about; the theme is what they have to say about it. The theme should be carried right through their text, with consistent emphasis, instead of merely stating it at the beginning and then forgetting it.

- Mmmm . . . my subject is "The Environment," and my theme is that preservation of the environment is essential if humans are to survive.

Having the topic under control: Whether writing fiction or nonfiction, the writer must have control over the ideas or information on the topic they are writing about in order to create meaningful text. Show the students how your statements are supported by evidence if writing a report, or how fiction is grounded in fact if writing a narrative:

- I'm not sure what a hippopotamus eats. I'll have to check that before I can start my story.
- I don't know much about this topic. Perhaps I'd better go to the library first or check the Internet and do some research. What are some questions I should try to answer?

Choosing the vocabulary: Writers choose vocabulary carefully and deliberately. This choice is directly influenced by the audience, purpose, and topic of the writing. Good writers tend to avoid clichés, "in" words, jargon, and euphemisms. Writers search for the appropriate word, cross out, re-write, or turn to a friend, a thesaurus, or a dictionary. They change words as the writing develops or as a different style becomes more appropriate, as well as when they re-read, edit, and proofread. Choice is limited by a writer's vocabulary, personal preference, and writing style. Note, however, that a writer's choice of words should not be limited by their inability to spell a word correctly. Spelling can be corrected later.

- This is a report, so I certainly won't start with "Once upon a time." How should I start? How about "Dinosaurs lived millions of years ago . . ." Yes, that sounds right.
- I'm writing a letter to a close friend that I haven't heard from for a while, so I can start informally with "Hi, stranger . . ."

Constructing sentences: Writers vary both the length and type of sentences they use. In general, short sentences are preferable to long ones, and simple sentences are preferable to complex ones. Again, the audience, purpose, and topic will determine choices of sentence construction.

- I can't have too many "ands." That's okay in direct speech, but not here. Perhaps I should break this sentence into three short ones. That will add emphasis and impact.
- If I put that phrase at the beginning of that sentence instead of in the middle, it will make the point much more strongly.

Clarifying ideas: Writers read and re-read, write and re-write, and often seek the advice of a supportive conference partner, as they polish their text and clarify their ideas. They continually go back to the intended audience and purpose to check that they are communicating effectively. They begin to read from the reader's perspective.

- Do you think this is really getting my point across? Do you think I should make this paragraph longer? What about this part? I was really having trouble there. Maybe I should make this sentence two short sentences. I wonder if I really need this bit—I will read it aloud and cut it out if I don't need it.

Proofreading: Once a writer is content that the piece of writing is conveying the intended meaning, it is time to proofread. This process also needs to be modeled. Proofreading involves re-reading the entire work in the light of its intended audience and purpose, slowly and carefully. The teacher can show how the proofreader edits for grammar, paragraphing, spelling, and punctuation. In order to ensure accuracy, proofreaders refer to dictionaries and thesauruses as well as other reference sources.

It is sometimes easier to proofread other people's writing than one's own because the writer is often too close to it and can no longer "see" what is actually there. To overcome this, some writers read from the bottom up and some read aloud and focus on each word. In an attempt to facilitate the proofreading process, writers often make notes for themselves as they draft their work. They put question marks over words that they cannot spell, make notes in the margin, and so on, as reminders to come back and fix something up. This is particularly true of spelling.

Getting the spelling right: There are several strategies that writers use to check their spelling that can also be modeled.

- Model the "spell-as-it-looks" strategy. Re-read your writing slowly and carefully and identify any words that don't look right.
- Write the words in different ways to see if any of the alternatives looks right. Writers often recognize the correct spelling once they see it.
- Model applying the "spell-as-it-means" strategy—that is, look for a root or base word that will indicate a meaning clue to the speller. For example, "exhibition" contains the word "exhibit."
- Apply the "spell-as-it-sounds" strategy by checking to see if the word is phonetically regular. Read the word aloud and check that the syllables pronounced match the letters in the word, such as sig-ni-fi-cant.
- Model looking around the room or in books for the correct spelling. This is only possible in a language-rich environment.
- Look up the word up in the dictionary, if you know the first three letters. If you don't, then try to think of other possible letters that make that sound.

Finally, we need to model strategies that help to identify wrong spellings and punctuation. Typically, these strategies include:

- reading the writing slowly and aloud, voice-pointing and looking at each word
- using a ruler to read one line at a time
- reading from the bottom up
- identifying words that look wrong
- saying the word slowly (pronouncing the syllables) to see if a part has been left out, e.g., sig-ni-fi-cant.

Using books as models: Books are full of demonstrations for writers— books can be used as models for genre, spellings, and layout. Model how you might use books as a model for writing. Set up the learning context so that students understand that there is a clear purpose to write the modeled genre. Students may work in pairs. Provide opportunities for students to discuss the purpose, audience, and topic as well as the features of the genre.

Model often: You will want to model often and might return to your draft over a period of time and model the process over time. Choose from the genres that students enjoy and need. The more you make explicit to your students exactly what goes on during the writing process, the more likely they are to become competent writers. The more you tune in to what your students are showing you that they need help with, the more likely they are to engage in your demonstrations.

Using students as models: Suggest that students model for each other. There is no reason why you should be seen as the only writer to emulate. Whenever a student writes particularly well or solves a problem that other students are struggling with invite them to model for the others. This could be one on one or in a small group.

As you model writing frequently in a variety of genres, expect your students' confidence as writers to increase. Praise them openly and often. Give useful, even constructively critical feedback. Provide opportunities for them to share their writing with as many people as you can.

Expect the standard of your students' writing to improve. Think up new ways to celebrate their developing craft.

Shared Writing

Shared writing is similar to modeled writing, and many of the above uses for modeled writing are also applicable here. The major difference is that with shared writing the responsibility for writing is shared between the teacher and the students. As such, shared writing is a joint construction of a piece of text of a particular genre in which the ideas come from both the teacher and the students. The teacher needs to be aware of the different parts of the writing process as well as how the genres and text features work and ensure that students are exposed to a variety of each. The teacher tends to keep the pen in his or her hand but will be drawing more information from the group than in modeled writing. Again, the lesson is focused and planned.

A shared writing session might begin like this:

"Today we will jointly construct an information report and later you can try writing your own about the sea creatures you have been researching. Who can help me get started here? What's the first thing we do in an information report? That's right—we need to jot down a few ideas, kind of like a plan. This will help us get our thoughts together before beginning . . . Okay, now we need a main heading. Who can suggest one? Now what comes next? Yes, we need an introduction. Can someone get us started?"

Again, the lesson will continue while engagement is high. The most common problem with shared writing is letting the lesson go too long and losing the focus. Sometimes it helps to allow the students to come and write the words, thus involving them more in the joint construction.

Guided Writing

Guided writing is most commonly used during the small group focus section of the writing workshop, but it can also be one-on-one. In the 1980s the notion of "the conference" was an important part of the writing process. It was a time set aside for the teacher and student to talk about the writing in progress. For the teacher it chiefly required the art of drawing forth ideas and fostering thinking by asking questions of the writer. The key to an effective conference was skillful teacher questioning based on an excellent knowledge of the writing process and the skills involved. We see little difference between the conference and a guided writing lesson.

In guided writing, the role of the teacher is to facilitate, guide, and respond to the student's thinking in the process of composing texts. Therefore, guided writing is when the students are constructing the text while being guided by the teacher. This is a useful strategy to focus on small group and/ or individual needs as identified through ongoing assessment. This strategy can be used to support a group of students not ready to write independently or alternatively used with a small group of students who would benefit from extension. In addition, it is an appropriate time to respond personally to an individual's writing. Skillful questioning of writers before giving advice is the key here. Through skillful questioning the teacher can ascertain the purpose, the audience, and the progress of the writing in order that the advice given is pertinent to the particular needs of that writer. When this happens within a small group, the other students can also question the writer, using the teacher's questions as a model. Such demonstrations of small group guided writing are the basis of helping or authors' circles.

While this strategy is being used it is likely that the remainder of the class would be writing independently. Below is an example of what a small group guided writing session for beginning writers might sound like. Matt is progressing well with his writing and is a good reader. The focus of this lesson is to give Matt the expectation that writing is something he has to think about and to strengthen the reading-writing connection. The purpose is also to involve the other group members in responding to another student's writing.

> The teacher begins, "I am going to write Matt's journal entry on this chart. Matt has done a terrific piece today. He wrote, 'On the weekend I went fishing. I had fun.' If this

was going to be written in a book like the ones we read, what could Matt do differently?" The teacher circles "On the weekend" and asks Matt exactly when he went fishing. After some talk the teacher might put a line under those words and write, "Early Saturday morning" over the top of them.

"That's a good beginning, Matt. It sounds like the first line from a book I have read. Has anyone got another question for Matt? Yes—'Who did you go with? And did you catch some fish?' I'd be interested to read that."

And so from a few minutes of talk Matt has many options for adding to his writing, including where they went, how long they were there, and so forth. Perhaps someone in the group might ask about the ending. "Why was it fun? Why do you like fishing so much?" The word "fun" as an ending would be a good word to explore, as it is used regularly as a quick ending by beginning writers. The teacher might lead the group to look at some endings in a selection of books and explore other words and ways to close a piece of writing.

Independent Writing

Students write independently to practice and apply the skills that they have learned though modeled, shared, and guided writing. It is essential that expectations and routines be clearly established and the students are supported appropriately during this time. The whole class focus and guided writing sessions continue to provide strong models of writing behaviors that support students when they write independently. Teachers should provide opportunities for sustained writing, which will involve all aspects of the writing process through to publishing.

The interpretation of the major teaching strategies represented on the model used throughout this book is simply a movement from instruction to use—a movement from teacher control to student control (see Figure 5.1 and Figure 7.3). It is important that the teacher finds a balance when using these strategies which will best meet the needs of the class and individual students.

Cameo: Teaching Kindergarteners about Audience

Background

It is week 8 in Term 1, and the twenty children in Ms. D's kindergarten are beginning to settle into the routines of school. There are five children in the class who come from non-English speaking backgrounds and have the support of the ESL teacher during the literacy block.

Time and Timing

Fifteen minutes is allocated to this activity at 11:00 a.m., after morning break.

Resources

The Jolly Postman (Ahlberg and Ahlberg 1986), chart paper, and marker pen.

Teaching Strategies

Modeled reading, shared writing, group sharing, independent writing

It is almost Easter, so Ms. D has decided to focus on writing a letter to the Easter Bunny. She begins with all the children sitting on the carpet in front of her. "Who knows what the Easter Bunny does?" she asks the children.

Hands go up. Montana is chosen and says, "He brings us Easter eggs." The children discuss the Easter Bunny for a few minutes.

"I wonder if the Easter Bunny will come to our class and bring us some Easter eggs," Ms. D says. "How can we make sure the Easter Bunny knows we want him to come? How would the Easter Bunny know where to come?"

These questions are posed as Ms. D shows the book *The Jolly Postman,* which has been read to the children several times before. "Maybe we could write a letter to invite the Easter Bunny."

Ms. D reminds the children about the letters in *The Jolly Postman* and pulls out the letter from Goldilocks. She reads it to the children and asks, "Why did Goldilocks write this letter to the Three Bears? What was Goldilocks' purpose for writing this letter?"

Sammy responds, "She is saying she is sorry and she wants to come and play."

"So if we want to ask the Easter Bunny to come to visit, how will we begin our letter?" Ms. D asks as she reaches for the marker pen.

Troy replies, "Dear Easter Bunny."

Ms. D begins to write, and as she does she thinks aloud.

"'Dear Easter . . .'—I have to write a capital letter for 'Easter' because it is a special name--'Bunny'--see? I have written another capital letter for 'Bunny' because he is a special person. Let's listen to Goldilocks' letter again." Ms. D reads the letter to the children again and adds, "What will we write next? Remember we want to invite the Easter Bunny to come visit us. How will we say that?" Turn to the person next to you and tell each other why you want the Easter Bunny to come to visit and how we can say that."

The children quickly turn to a partner and sit "eye-to-eye and knee-to-knee," an organizational strategy the children use often. There is a buzz as the children talk about the Easter Bunny, Easter eggs, and chocolate. Ms. D moves around the pairs and bends over to listen. She returns to her chair out the front and reiterates, "So, what will we write in our letter?"

Hands go up, and Ms. D chooses Ryan. "Please can you come to our school?"

Ms. D begins to write. "'Please . . .' I have to write a capital 'P' because it is the first word in our sentence 'can' I know some people know how to write 'can.' Write it in the air so I can see it." Some children do this as Ms. D writes "can." "'. . . you come . . .' what does 'come' begin with?" Children call out "c." '. . . to our school . . .'--we have 'school' written somewhere in this room. Jack, go and bring that word." Jack walks to the door and brings the label over that says, "Lima Public School." "Jack, can you copy the word from the sign?" Jack takes the marker pen and copies 'Lima Public School."

Ms. D asks the children to read the text from the beginning:

"Dear Easter Bunny,
Please can you come to our Lima Public School?"

Elise says, "That doesn't make sense. It has to say, 'come to Lima Public School.'" Ms. D hands her the pen and asks her to cross out "our." They all read it again and agree that it now makes more sense. Ms. D adds a question mark, explaining that this is needed because "we are asking a question."

Ms. D asks the children to stand up and read their letter again. They do so with great gusto. "Now, why do we want the Easter Bunny to come to our school?" she asks. "Tell your partner why we want the Easter Bunny to come." More pair talk fills the room.

Lam is asked to share what he and his partner decided. Lam begins, "Easter eggs."

Ms. D asks, "Will we write just 'Easter eggs'?" And she reads the letter again.

Lam's partner responds with, "Please can you bring us some eggs?"

Ms. D begins to write. "'Please . . .' we have written that before so spell it for me." The children call out the letters c·a·n as she writes them. She passes the pen to Raphael and asks him to write "can." "Good," Ms. D comments as she points to "can," then adds, "'You'—we know how to write 'you,' don't we?" She passes the pen to Ellie, saying, "We have 'you' here" while pointing to "you" in the first sentence. They stop and re·read the sentence again.

"'Please can you . . .' what next?"

Lam replies, "Bring us some eggs." Ms. D senses the children are getting tired, so she writes the words, saying them as she writes. They all read the letter from the beginning and then Sammy says, "You have to have a question mark." He comes up and draws the question mark.

"Have we finished?" Ms. D asks. "Will the Easter Bunny know who wrote the letter?"

Montana says quietly, "We have to say, 'Love from Ms. D's Class'." Ms. D passes her the pen, and she comes and writes this.

The children proudly read the letter again. Ms. D tears off the chart paper and pins it up on the display board, saying "The Easter Bunny will know who sent the letter and why we want him to come. Now we have to wait to see if he does."

Reflection on This Instruction

In setting up and carrying out this task, Ms. D considered time and timing. She considered the resources needed, and she utilized several teaching strategies. Predominately she used a modeled writing strategy and at times moved into shared writing. The students were engaged and the lesson continued for about fifteen to twenty minutes.

Ms. D's purpose at the whole text level was to model how to write a letter of invitation. She made the connection to a letter in the book, *The Jolly Postman,* which had been read to the class several times. Ms. D clearly identified for the children the purpose and audience for their letter and returned to these often.

Ms. D focused at the sentence level by making explicit the structure of the sentence that was most appropriate to achieve the purpose for the audience of the Easter Bunny. She introduced the terms "question" and "question mark."

Finally, Ms. D focused the children's attention on the word level by making explicit the capital letter and the spelling of words. In doing so Ms. D not only modeled the strategy of "sounding out" but also copying the words that are known to be in the room.

Throughout Ms. D was assessing the children's levels of understanding and their engagement while noting each child's developing knowledge at the whole text, sentence, and word levels.

A follow up on this lesson may be that some children choose to write a personal letter to the Easter Bunny. By leaving the chart for all to see, Ms. D ensures that the children can use it to copy words they need or the whole text if necessary.

Cameo: Teaching Grade 4 Students about the Genre of Reports

Background

The 24 Grade 4 students had been learning about small creatures in science. They had been reading information reports and had been analyzing the texts, discussing how these were written. On this day Mr. G asked the students to write their own information report. He was aware that the children had been introduced to information reports in Grade 3, so he expected that they had a basic knowledge of the genre. The written texts the children would produce would allow him to assess the children's current knowledge and inform future teaching experiences. The small creature for today's task was the frog.

Time and Timing

The writing task was scheduled for approximately thirty minutes in the time allocated to science. The children had been studying the unit on small creatures for several weeks. The focus had been on general information, life cycle, appearance, and habitat. They had already explored information about spiders, butterflies, and small lizards.

Resources

Five information books on frogs (three of one title and one each of two other titles; all were within the children's reading ability), chart paper, and marker pens.

Teaching Strategies

Modeled reading, shared writing, group sharing, group writing

Mr. G reminds the children about their previous work on small creatures. He tells the students he is going to divide them in to five groups so they can work together on their "new small creature." Mr. G moves around the class and gives each child a number, 1 through 5.

"Okay, all the number 1s can move over here," says Mr. G, pointing to a spot on the carpet at the front of the room. He organizes the other four groups into various spaces in the room, giving each group a piece of paper and a marker pen. He tells the children, "First each group needs to pick a scribe and a reporter." Once this is done Mr. G announces, "Today we are going to discuss a new small creature—the frog. Now on your paper I want each group to write down all the things you know already about frogs. Don't worry too much about spelling at this point. I will give you five minutes for you to write as many 'things' or facts that you already know about frogs."

The children begin their task and Mr. G moves among the groups, responding to questions or comments. He observes all groups before he asks the children to stop work.

"Wow! I can see that you already know a great deal about frogs," he says. "I am going to ask each group reporter to share what you did. As your reporter shares, I will write your facts on my large chart."

Group 1's reporter stands with the group's sheet and reads, "They live in water and on land. Amphibians. They hop. Slimy." Mr. G writes and the list grows.

"Great!" says Mr. G. "Group 2 reporter, please only share new information. If we already have the facts on the chart, don't tell us again."

And so group share continues until all groups have given their known information. The list is quite long and impressive, and the children are very excited about their combined list.

"You sure know a great deal about frogs," Mr. G tells the class as he writes the heading, "What we already know about frogs" at the top of the chart.

Holding up the information books, he says, "I have some books here that are about frogs. Each group will get one book, so you to need sit in a circle on the floor so you can see the book. Pass the book around and each one of you can read a page out loud. Remember to also look at the pictures and illustrations because they give facts, too. Now here is the clever part. As you do this, think about any *new* facts that you find. They have to be facts that we don't already have on our charts. Jot these on your paper."

The children work in their groups, reading, talking, and writing. Mr. G moves among the groups, observing the children. Occasionally he stops to talk to a group, but mostly he observes, making notes of how individual children read, interact, and so on.

After ten minutes Mr. G stops the groups and asks the reporters to identify any new facts. These he writes on a new piece of chart paper labeled, "New facts we have learned."

Once this list is complete, Mr. G uses the following questions to guide discussion about the facts now listed on the two charts:

- What facts are general information?
- What facts are about appearance?
- What facts are about the life cycle?
- What facts are about the frog's habitat?

"We have so many facts now that we can write our own information reports," he informs the class. "Remember that we have been reading information reports. And you have a model of how these are written in your book. So let's think first about how an information report begins. What information comes first?"

Dillon is quick to respond, "A general statement."

"That's right. So let's think of a general statement that you could use for your information report." Hands go up and Mr. G selects several students to share their general statement. He moves to the chalkboard and writes the heading, "Frogs."

"Let's combine two of the general statements you have given me." He writes, "Frogs are amphibians. That means they live in water and on land."

Mr. G goes to the two charts created earlier and puts a line under these two facts.

"What could come next?" "What other facts have we?" he asks while pointing to the charts. "Now each group can complete their own information report. You can use this general statement, or you might have another way of starting. Remember you should organize your facts under the headings of appearance, habitat, and life cycle."

The children huddle in their groups, talking about what to write as Mr. G hands each group a clean piece of paper.

"Remember this is a draft. You can add illustrations and images later."

The groups begin their writing. There is much discussion about sentence structure, word choice, spelling, and punctuation. The children refer often to the charts and to their book. Mr. G moves among the groups, observing, asking questions, clarifying, and generally supporting the collaborative writers. After ten minutes Mr. G stops the groups and asks one member of each group to come up to the front with the group's writing. Each reporter shares what has been written so far. The children spontaneously applaud at the end of each reading.

Mr. G collects the groups' drafts and asks the children to go back to their tables. "Tomorrow," he says, "you can continue working on these in writers' workshop."

Reflection on This Instruction

Mr. G's purposes for this lesson were many. At the whole text level he wanted to know if the children not only knew what the information report genre "looked like," namely, its purpose and grammatical features, but whether they could write in such a genre. He wanted to assess the children's ability to read and use informational texts as well as know that they could use written texts as models for their own writing.

An important consideration Mr. G wanted his students to understand was that when writing such texts one must have control over the facts that are to be included in the text. Personal background knowledge is important, but it needs to be checked with the more authoritative resources on the subject. Mr. G also wanted the children to be aware that much of the information can be gleaned from "reading" the illustrations and images in the reference materials supplied.

Time and timing were important in this scenario. Mr. G deliberately chose the time in the schedule allocated to science, as he wanted the children to understand that reading and writing in science involve particular genres of writing. Mr. G also had prepared the children for this task by examining other small creatures and texts written about them.

The choice of appropriate reference materials was critical. Choosing several different books allowed for cross-checking of information. And choosing books at the children's reading levels meant that they knew they could return to them for future reference.

The teaching strategies Mr. G used in this scenario were many and moved from teacher directed to teacher supported to independent (albeit collaboratively independent), back to teacher directed, and so on. And throughout the lesson Mr. G had many opportunities to observe and listen to individual students, assessing their knowledge and skills in literacy at the whole text level as well as the sentence and word levels. He finished the lesson by telling the children what the follow up to this lesson would be.

PILLAR 4: ASSESSMENT OF WRITING

The teachers' opportunities to assess their students throughout the above two cameos were many. Actually knowing what to assess, how to collect information, and how to store and analyze such information are constant challenges for teachers. We believe it to be so important that we have devoted Chapter 8 to the fourth pillar: Assessment of Writing.

Chapter 8: Assessing Writing Using a Teaching/Learning Cycle

Assessment and evaluation are a critical part of the teaching/learning cycle—be it the teaching of writing, reading, or any other content area. Put simply, we assess, we plan, and we teach, and these processes overlap and continue. The process is not linear—that is, assessment does not simply happen at the end of any teaching enterprise. Rather, assessment occurs throughout teaching, although we are not always conscious of it at the time. Figure 8.1 demonstrates the role of assessment in our daily teaching and learning practices. We want to stress that while we will discuss this model in relation to writing it is applicable to all teaching and learning.

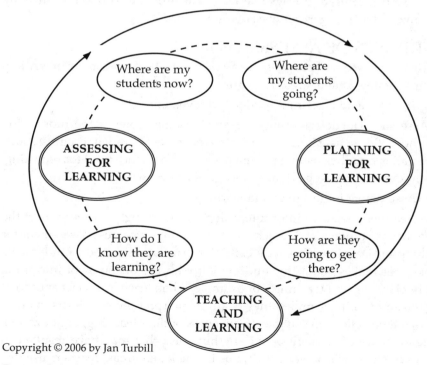

Figure 8.1: A teaching/learning cycle

There are many stakeholders who have an interest or "stake" in the assessment of students. Each of these stakeholders requires or needs something different from the assessment process. The following list identifies the most obvious stakeholders and their needs:

- Education decision makers need to ensure that schools are delivering quality education
- School leaders need to ensure that there is quality teaching and learning in the schools for which they are responsible
- Parents need to be certain that they are receiving reliable information about their children's progress
- Students need feedback that will enable them to reflect on their learning and to set goals for their future learning
- Teachers need to ensure that students remain the central focus in their classrooms
- Teachers need to know that their approaches and strategies are meeting the needs of all students.

Valid and reliable information is necessary to inform all these stakeholders and must be acquired in ways that lead to as little interruption to the daily teaching and learning experiences as is possible.

PURPOSES OF ASSESSMENT

There are two main purposes for assessment—be it assessment of writing, reading, or any content area. They are:

- To accurately determine student achievement.

Assessment for determining student achievement refers to the information a teacher collects that allows judgments to be made on student progress. Such information and the ensuing judgments are the evidence used for reporting. This information must be rigorous and valid as we will explain.

- Assessment for teaching and learning.

Assessment needs to inform teaching and learning in order to meet the needs of the students and to achieve curriculum outcomes. Assessment for teaching and learning refers to the collection of information and the judgments the teacher makes about this information with the purposes of informing future planning and teaching. For example, when teachers collect anecdotal records and writing samples, they begin to interpret these artifacts in order to assist their reflections on the effectiveness of their teaching, organization, content, choice of strategies, and anything else that may have resulted in improved standards of work or decline in particular areas. Teachers use this information to reflect and ultimately make plans for the next wave of their teaching. This form of assessment is based on a belief that acknowledges the skills, knowledge, and responsibility of the teacher in this process. In brief, assessment for teaching should result in optimal learning for all.

Keeping these purposes in mind is critical in determining the kind of assessment that will take place and in ensuring that the teaching/learning cycle is in place in the classroom. Too often we embrace assessment ideas or strategies and never stop to determine whether the particular strategy will provide the kind of information that will make a difference to the future learning of all students.

A WRITING ASSESSMENT MODEL

The assessment of writing is underpinned by all the principles discussed above. Designing assessment procedures to appraise particular aspects of the teaching and learning of writing can take a variety of forms. It is important to select reliable assessment activities that will be part of the on-going learning experience as often as possible. Information can be collected across all phases of teaching and learning writing, including the whole text, sentence, and word levels (see Chapter 1). This information can be collected through observations, discussions, and anecdotal records as well as analysis of work samples. Collecting multiple types of information via many sources allows teachers to use this information to cross check the judgments they make about student learning. Such judgments can be considered to be more valid and reliable than a judgment made on a single piece of information, such as that taken from a single test.

For instance, Mr. V, a kindergarten teacher, observed a group of four boys talking when they should have been writing. His first judgment was that the boys were wasting time and he should tell them to get on with their work. However, he realized that he should collect more information before making such a judgment. Mr. V moved to the group and inquired what they were doing. They each had their paper and pencils but had not begun to write. They were, however, using a separate piece of paper to work out how to spell "Disneyland." They explained that Justin, one of the boys in the group, was going to Disneyland during the holidays, and they were helping him work out how to write the word. A closer look at the page where all their attempts had been made demonstrated to Mr. V that they had indeed been working. As a group they had almost worked out the spelling of the word, and he could see that they knew to break the word into two parts—"Disney" and "land." The latter they had spelled correctly, and the former after several attempts was almost correct—"Disny." This example demonstrates that gaining multiple pieces of information gave Mr. V rich information that meant that the judgments he made about the boys learning were both valid and reliable. Decisions about future teaching made by Mr. V could also be considered to be more reliable.

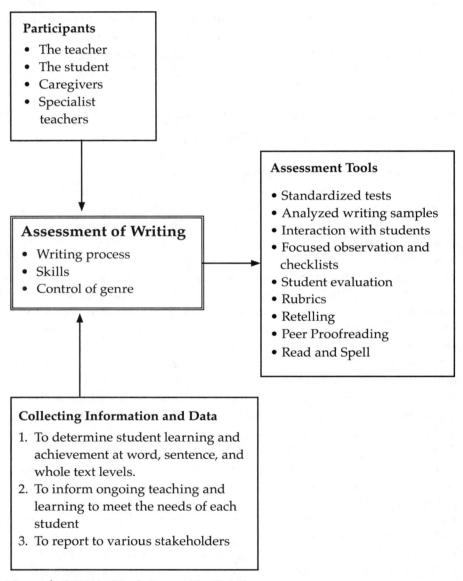

Participants

- The teacher
- The student
- Caregivers
- Specialist teachers

Assessment of Writing

- Writing process
- Skills
- Control of genre

Assessment Tools

- Standardized tests
- Analyzed writing samples
- Interaction with students
- Focused observation and checklists
- Student evaluation
- Rubrics
- Retelling
- Peer Proofreading
- Read and Spell

Collecting Information and Data

1. To determine student learning and achievement at word, sentence, and whole text levels.
2. To inform ongoing teaching and learning to meet the needs of each student
3. To report to various stakeholders

Figure 8.2: A writing assessment model

Figure 8.2 is a visual representation of the specifics of assessing writing. Participants in this process include not only the teacher and students but also the children's parents or caregivers and the specialist teachers who work with the students. In what follows we will outline in more detail the components of this model.

Collecting Information and Data

Knowing what and how to collect information or data as well as when to collect it is a constant challenge for teachers. This seems even more so with writing. In the past we tended to make judgments only on the final product, and while this is one form of data it is by no means the only form or even the most important.

Anthony et al. developed a framework for data collection that they called "the quad"—a circle divided by two crossing lines that produced four quarters. They labeled each quarter with these categories: observation of process, observation of product, classroom measures, and decontextualized measures (1991, 30-33).

Observation of process includes:

- Anecdotal comments from classroom observation and reflection of students throughout the writing process
- Interviews/conferences with students, parents, and other professionals who may teach the students about the various aspects of writing
- Responses to reading: written retellings, text reconstruction.

Observations of product include:

- Published pieces
- Drafts
- Notes and entries made in learning journals, diaries, and other workbooks
- Writing logs that record what has been written and the purpose and audience for that writing
- Reading logs, including responses to readings.

Classroom measures include:

- Text-related activities that the teacher assigns a grade or score
- Teacher-made units and assessment tasks.

Decontextualized measures include:

- Criterion reference measures
- District or cross-grade tests
- State and national tests.

Anthony et al. note, however, that each quarter of the quad need not be equal. What is critical is that teachers identify a "particular weight" to be allocated to each of the segments and suggest that even within a given school year the balance may need to change. For instance, in our state, New South Wales, students in Grades 3 and 5 sit for a state-wide literacy criterion-referenced writing test. This decontextualized measure requires teachers to spend some time preparing their students to write a piece prescribed by the test procedures, also known as "one-shot writing." Teachers know that the children will also be asked to write using two specific genres, one fiction and one nonfiction. So the balance for these grade levels as the test date comes closer will tend to have a greater focus on classroom and decontextualized measures, as it would be unfair for the students not to have some experience with writing in test-like conditions. Besides, they need to understand that such "one-shot" writing has a specific purpose and audience and is therefore a different form of writing from that which they may do in class. In a Grade 1 class, however, the teacher is likely to have a greater focus on observation of process and product that will not change over the year.

It should be remembered that this framework functions largely as a management system. As Anthony et al. remind us, "Teachers should not be enslaved by the collection of data. Rather the framework should allow teachers to collect data systematically" (1991, 35). When teachers use this framework they certainly become more conscious of what it means to balance their collection of assessment data. Information about writers and their writing can be collected in a number of ways. It may be collected on a cyclic basis to ensure that all students are regularly observed. Each week the teacher might select four or five students for particular focus during the writing workshop. Using this type of organization, students are regularly observed and their respective work samples collected.

Alternatively a teacher might design specific "tasks" at various points in the teaching/learning cycle to collect information. These tasks can be complex or simple. For example, a retelling can provide rich information about control of structure and use of grammar and punctuation and spelling at the whole text, sentence, and word level. Used in conjunction with a rubric, this assessment process allows students to be involved and set themselves goals for continued learning.

Similarly, the writing task may take the form of a follow-up activity to some previous learning experience. The "Certificate of Appreciation" in Figure 8.3 is a good example. The students in this Grade 2 class had invited visitors to their classroom to talk about what they did in the community. At the same time they had been introduced to the various forms of writing that could be used to show their appreciation: both certificates and thank-you notes were modeled to this class of seven and eight year olds. Once modeled it became an independent assessment task as well as a purposeful writing activity for the children to complete. The teacher was interested in collecting information on how well the students had listened to the guest speakers, which would be indicated by the accuracy of information in the writing, the control the student had over the form of writing selected (whole text level), and the various skills and strategies of spelling, punctuation, and grammar (sentence and word levels) applied by the student. In addition, the writing had a very specific purpose and audience in that on completion the certificates would be mailed to the guests. This is an excellent example of a purposeful piece of writing that provides a range of assessment data.

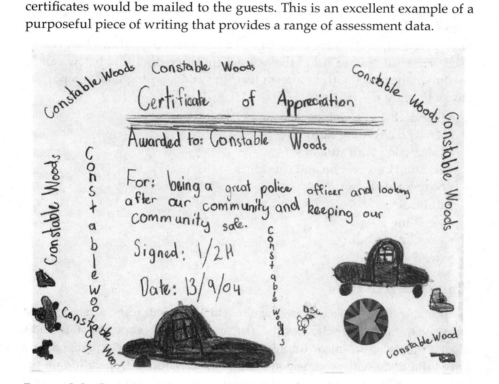

Figure 8.3: Certificate of Appreciation by Jasmine and Lucy

Storing Data

Before moving on to discuss the various assessment tools we can use to assess writing, we need to mention the importance of storing the collected data or information. All information and work samples collected should be dated and carefully stored for future use. Future use may include reporting to parents and caregivers or showing students the progress they have made over time. Student workbooks can serve as storage places. It is a good idea at the start of the school year to select the first piece that children write. This should be dated, photocopied, and carefully stored for comparison as the year unfolds. Collecting samples of writing approximately every six to ten weeks works well for many teachers and their students.

ASSESSMENT TOOLS FOR WRITING

We believe that the nature and procedures of assessment should be a whole-school approach so that learning occurs as a continuum and each year the learning is built on with a spiraling effect. When this occurs, teachers can track student progress more accurately and consistently. A whole-school approach would ensure that writing is being judged by the same set of criteria each year. There is a range of assessment procedures that can be used across all grades. All of the assessment strategies listed below can be used to gather data both to inform teaching and learning and to report on student progress.

- Standardized tests
- Analyzed writing samples
- Interaction with students
- Focused observation and checklists
- Student evaluation
- Rubrics
- Retelling
- Peer Proofreading
- Read and Spell.

Standardized Tests

There are few places now where standardized tests are not used extensively. Some are school wide, district wide, and many are state wide. Most of these tests have limitations, as they are decontextualized and have little to do with what is going on in the classroom. Depending on the test, the results, analyzed carefully, might give insights into an aspect of a student's learning that will serve to provide new information or triangulate data already collected. However, teachers need to guard against making assumptions on test results that go beyond the scope of the test. In our opinion, the most common problem with standardized tests is their use in comparing schools and districts. Standardized tests of writing can focus only on the product, and then only at the sentence and word levels. We concur with other researchers (for example, Anthony et al. 1991 and Kohn 1999) that standardized tests have little to do with quality classroom teaching. They may serve the purposes of the politicians and administrators, but in the main they do not provide enough data to inform future learning experiences for students.

Analysis of Writing Samples

Analysis of writing samples offers a reliable way to assess aspects of students' writing at the word, sentence, and whole text levels. When analyzing writing, teachers should pay attention to the students' skills and strategies, control of the process, ability to meet the needs of audience and purpose, control of the genre, and to the general quality of the piece of writing. In brief, the teacher assesses the process *and* the product. The information collected should form the basis of future planning and teaching. The following example demonstrates how a Grade 1 teacher assessed a student's control of both process and product over a period of time.

Assessing Product and Process for Matt

The piece in Figure 8.4 was written by a seven year old after a trip to the zoo. The writing task involved using the genre of recount. The students had learned the structure of a recount and had engaged in a discussion about what they had seen at the zoo prior to commencing independent writing. Figure 8.4 is a typed version of the writing with spelling unchanged. The student, Matt, has a love for animals and had been to the zoo many times prior to the school visit. The length of the piece indicated that on this occasion, Matt had a great deal to recount, so the writing seems to have come easily. It is a good example of a student who has control of content as well as structure. In other words, because Matt had a lot of knowledge about the topic, his attention could go to the structure of the piece rather than struggling with what to write. A detailed analysis at the whole text, sentence, and word levels follows in the table in Figure 8.5

While this student is achieving well with his writing, an important part of the process of annotating writing is for the teacher to ask, where each student should go to next. In this case, a guided writing session with a focus on adding detail would be a good place to start in order to continue Matt's writing development. It would also be appropriate to engage Matt in further editing, and this could be achieved partly by providing a clearer audience and purpose for the writing. It could also be done by selecting one or two students writing at a similar level and teaching the group the editing skills. All of these interventions should be conducted in a way that affirms the success of this young writer so that it moves him forward with his learning about writing.

Recount: Trip to the Zoo[1]

On Tuesday I went to (the) Taronga Zoo with all of the year ones. First we had moning tea then after that we went to the toilet. After that we saw some anamels. We saw the spider (moh) monkes and the seals. (a) The person that was the boss of my group was Mrs Brynt. After the anamels I saw I went to the Bird Show. My favret bird was the Black cokatoo. I liked it because I liked the noise. I had lunch while I watched it. It was alot of fun.

After the Bird Show I saw some more anamels. I saw the giraffes and the zebrars and the (gril) chimpanzees. Then we went to the Education Center. (and) We had a leson there. I got to hold a fasmid and while we were there we saw a Shingle back lazed. It was (colud) cold becase it's a reptile. This mite (sona) sound a bit funny becase we needed help (get in) getting to the Education Centre. When we got there I saw a pekoks (tale) tail fethers. It looked a bit funny. After that we went Backyad to Bush. First I saw a bee hive I only had a short go becase there was a long line. Then I saw some bugs. Then I went into another room and I saw a red back in a (c) jar. Then I went outside and I saw a red back in a twolit it was full of web. We made (or) our way back to the bus and we got on and went back to school. I had lots and lots and lots and lots of fun.

---

[1] Note: the parentheses indicate words crossed out or written over by Matt

Figure 8.4: Recount of a visit to the zoo by Matt

	What Matt Can Do	Teacher's Comments
Whole text level	Can write a recount	Retells his outing to the zoo in great detail
	Begins with an orientation	On Tuesday I went to (the) Taronga Zoo with all of the year ones
	Keeps to topic all through piece	Clear to reader what Matt did, who he met, and what he saw
	Sequence of events clear	It is clear what happened first, second, and so on
	Re-reads and edits writing to maintain meaning	On Tuesday I went to (the) Taronga Zoo with all of the year ones. Crossed out "the" because it didn't make sense.
	Comments on events at appropriate places	My favret bird was the Black cokatoo This mite (sona) sound a bit funny
	Knows to have an "ending"	We made (or) way back to the bus and we got on and went back to school. I had lots and lots and lots and lots of fun.
Sentence level	Writes in past tense and maintains this throughout	Went, had, saw, etc.
	Uses connectives	Then, after that, first, and while
	Has the concept of a sentence	All sentences have a verb and begin with capital letter
	Subject/verb agreement evident	We saw, I had
Word level	Has control over many spelling patterns and attempts are close	Becose, miote, zebrars
	Spells high-frequency words correctly	We, were, saw
	Uses references (wall charts, dictionary) to check words	Shingle back lizard, Education Centre

Figure 8.5: Analysis of Matt's recount

Figure 8.6 is an example of descriptive writing by the same student twelve months later. This genre gives the young writer an opportunity to demonstrate reading-writing connections, as it appears he has borrowed some structures from some of his reading. He has good control of the genre "literary description." As a first draft he demonstrates excellent spelling skills, spelling more complex patterns such as "identifying" and "unknown" correctly. His choice of adjectives is imaginative, and he paints a vivid picture of his character. His use of complex phrases such as "big landing thumps" and "soft flying sounds" add action to his description.

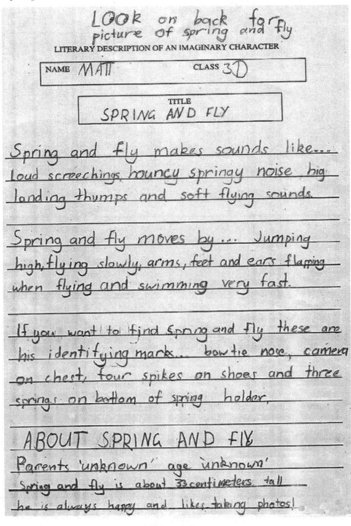

Figure 8.6: "Spring and Fly" by Matt

Where to next? Once again, participation in a helping circle will provide a sense of audience. Matt now needs opportunities to begin writing more sustained pieces for specific audiences and purposes to continue the development of his writing skills and to ensure that his interest is maintained.

Interaction with Students

Talking to children about their writing reveals key information about the strategies they use and their understanding of the writing process. Such interaction needs to be triggered by careful questions posed by the teacher. For instance eight-year-old Nicole loved to write and seemed to have control over a variety of genres. However, her spelling often left her teacher speechless. In one piece Nicole had spelled "truck" four different ways—"truk," "trucke," "truch," and "truck." When asked why she had done this, she responded, "That's what I am supposed to do." Further discussion unraveled the mystery. At some point Nicole had heard her teacher say, "If you are not sure how to spell a word, try to write it several ways." What Nicole has misunderstood was she was to do this in her spelling journal, not in her writing piece. When asked which spelling was the correct form, she quickly pointed to "truck." Careful questioning can get inside children's heads and reveal *how* they are learning as well as *what* they are learning.

Focused Observation and Checklists

Observing students when they are writing will allow the teacher to collect information related to the process of writing that, in addition to analyzing the product, will give him or her a fuller picture of the student's control over writing. Field notes and anecdotal records can be collected quickly as the teacher moves about the writing workshop. The purpose is to collect information that will not be evident in the finished piece. Did the writer struggle to begin? Did the writer refer to resources? Which ones? Was there an indication of enjoyment? What did "enjoyment" look like? Was there evidence of struggle? Did the writer use scaffolds or other supports available in the classroom?

A variety of checklists can be developed (see below for examples) to guide teacher observation or to guide students in their writing and to support them throughout all stages of the process from selecting a genre based on audience and purpose through to the final product. A checklist may include comments on general aspects of the writer's behavior such as *enjoys writing, participates readily, has a good sense of audience, can gather information, edits and*

Teacher Checklist—The Process of Writing

Name _____ Grade _____ Date_____

The Writing Process	Comment
Focusing Has the student identified an audience and purpose for the writing? Has the student selected an appropriate genre? Has the student engaged in any planning before commencing to write? Has the student collected and organized information? Has the student maintained the focus?	
Composing Is the student willing to write? Does the student have spelling strategies to create a text? Does the student have knowledge of text structure to create a text?	
Editing Is the student willing to edit? Can the student adopt the stance of a reader to identify points where meaning is lost or information is incomplete? Can the student refine meaning and make choices between different ways of saying the same thing?	
Proofreading Can the student identify non-standard spelling and grammar? Can the student correct identified errors? Is the student applying a range of spelling strategies? Is the student using punctuation, sentence, and paragraph conventions appropriately?	
Publishing Can the student think back to the audience and purpose and determine the form of publishing that is appropriate?	

Original form copyright © 1997 by Wendy Bean and Chrystine Bouffler; current form © 2006 by Wendy Bean

Figure 8.7: Teacher Checklist: The Process of Writing (adapted from Bean and Bouffler 1997, 73)

proofreads effectively, can write particular kinds of text, and so on. On the other hand, checklists can be specific and relate more closely to aspects of the product such as control of genre (whole text level), grammar (sentence level), spelling, spelling strategies, and punctuation (word level). To the extent that there are certain learning goals that are common for all students, checklists can provide the teacher with a quick way of gathering information on the achievement related to those goals.

However, we strongly suggest that a checklist is most effective when it responds to the teaching and learning that is taking place in the classroom. Therefore, it is our opinion that a published checklist will always need modifications. We have included a range of checklists below and in the appendix for teachers to consider with the hope that teachers will adapt these to suit their particular context and students' needs.

When the questions in the checklist in Figure 8.7 are examined, it becomes clear that process and product are highly interrelated. It is also obvious that it is of little value addressing problems of editing and proofreading until the learner has some measure of control over focusing and composing.

Since all language is context specific, judgments about writing need to be made in the light of what we know about those contexts. Some judgments, therefore, need to be made about topic, audience, purpose, and genre. The checklist in Figure 8.8, with a focus on product, may be useful for these purposes.

The questions on the checklist in Figure 8.8, also shown in Appendix 2, may assist the teacher to stay focused and help to clarify how the learner has succeeded as a writer. However, they will not provide the full picture. There will also be questions about quality of writing that the teacher needs to articulate to students and ultimately assess. As we said in Chapter 1, there is no simple way of determining quality. In Chapter 1, we challenged our readers to take the time to consider the question, "What makes writing good?" because we believe that it is difficult to make judgments about the quality of writing until teachers go through the process of making explicit their criteria for what they perceive "good" writing to be.

Teacher Checklist—The Product of Writing

Name _____ Grade _____ Date _____

Writing Product	Comment
Topic Is the topic appropriate to the audience? Is there sufficient information or are there things the reader still needs to know? Are the ideas or events properly sequenced? Is there coherence (related to the genre)? Are the ideas original? Are they presented originally? (Retelling and modeling may be encouraged, but copying the work of others—plagiarism—should be discouraged.)	
Audience Who is the audience? Is the subject matter appropriate to the audience? Is the language appropriate to the audience? Is the presentation appropriate to the audience? • spelling • punctuation • grammar • handwriting • layout Has the writing been edited and proofread? Are spelling, punctuation, and grammar appropriate?	
Purpose What was the purpose of the writing? Was it achieved? Did the writing entertain, inform, persuade, make comparisons, record observations, clarify thinking, predict, or hypothesize, depending on the genre?	
Genre Is the student in control of the text form? Is the control full or partial? Can the student structure and sustain a narrative, report, letter, or play, or does the structure break down? Which genre has the student made use of?	

Original form copyright © 1997 by Wendy Bean and Chrystine Bouffler; current form © 2006 by Wendy Bean

Figure 8.8: Example of Teacher Checklist: The Product of Writing (adapted from Bean and Bouffler 1997, 73)

Student Writing Checklist #1

Name: A Visit to the Zoo by Matt

Date: June 8

Purpose of my writing: To recount my zoo trip

Audience for my writing: My Mum and Dad who didn't go

Genre selected: Recount

My writing makes sense.
> I have read my writing out loud. ✓
> I have checked if there is anything I need to add or to take out. ✓

Spelling
> I have circled the words that I need to check for correct spelling.
> I changed some spelling
> I have looked for the correct spelling:
> * on the word walls ✓
> * in a dictionary
> * in my word list. ✓

Punctuation
> I have checked I have used capital letters and periods. ✓
> I have checked I have used commas, question marks, and speech marks correctly. ✓

> I am ready for a conference. Yes

Figure 8.9: Matt's self-assessment checklist

Student Self-assessment

Assisting learners to keep their own checklists, rubrics, learning journals, and writing logs encourages self-assessment. The aim is to develop a metalanguage for students to use as they reflect on and respond to their own learning. This will develop over time through teacher modeling and the use of these tools. Eventually the goal is to jointly construct rubrics and checklists with the class once they have knowledge of these tools, their purpose, and the language to talk about their learning. Well-designed rubrics and checklists are useful additions to a student portfolio to provide specific information about progress in writing.

Each example in this section is appropriate for different grade levels, and each has a slightly different purpose. These models can be used by teachers to develop their own checklists that are appropriate to the students in their

Student Writing Checklist #2

1. Does your writing make sense? Hints: • Who is the audience for this piece of writing? • What was the purpose of the writing? • Do the events or facts follow each other in proper order or are some parts jumbled? • Are there any parts you need to add or cut?	
2. Is your spelling correct? Proofread your writing and circle the words that you think may be spelled incorrectly. Hint: • To check your spelling, use a ruler to uncover your text and read line-by-line, paying attention to each word. To find the correct spelling, refer to a dictionary, word lists in the room, or a book where you remember seeing the word.	
3. Is each sentence a complete thought that begins with a capital letter and ends with a period? Hint: • Go back and read your writing out loud quietly to check that the whole piece sounds right. You will be able to hear where the sentences begin and end.	
4. Is your punctuation correct? Check that you have used capital letters and that commas, periods, question marks, and quotation marks are in the correct place. Hints: • Have you used a capital letter for people's names or places? • Are there sentences that ask a question? Do they end with a question mark? • Do you have characters talking in your writing? Have you used quotation marks? • Is the paragraphing correct?	
5. Is your use of grammar correct? Hints: • Are nouns, pronouns, and verbs in agreement? • Is your use of tense correct and consistent?	
6. Is your handwriting clear and are your letters well formed? Hint: • Neat handwriting will help whoever reads your writing to enjoy and understand what you have written.	

Figure 8.10: Complex student writing checklist (adapted from Bean 2000, 8)

grade. The checklist in Figure 8.9 was completed by Matt, whose writing we discussed in the cameo earlier in this chapter. Figure 8.10 is an example of a student checklist for more proficient writers.

Self-assessment relies heavily on the students' ability to reflect on their learning. However, in our experience, students do not necessarily know how to reflect in this way unless they have been taught through modeling and oral discussion. They need to learn a language to use when they are reflecting. Carefully worded questions are helpful to guide reflection. In the early years regular modeling of purposeful reflection on learning is essential.

The two short personal reflections in Figures 8.11 and 8.12 on writing were written toward the end of the school year by Grade 4 students who had had many experiences throughout the year using personal checklists and rubrics.

As a writer I have had good and bad experiences.
A good one was when I finished "What is a rainbow?"
A bad one was when I had a mind blank and couldn't think of anything.
I have enjoyed writing.

Figure 8.11: Reflection on writing by Jordan

My experience of being a writer is that it is great to write. Its fun and it lets your emagination run wild. It would be one of my dreams to be a writter like my anty and grandma. It has been fun because I have now learn to write really well. My favourite text type is Report.

Figure 8.12: Reflection on writing by Kelsey

Rubric for Exposition Writing—Grade 2

Name _____ Date _____

Criteria	3	2	1	Student	Teacher
Structure	I used the correct structure for my exposition. • I began with a clear opening statement. • I wrote several reasons for or against the topic. • I ended my writing by stating my position.	I did not include all the structures needed for an exposition.	I did not use the correct structure when I wrote my exposition.		
Punctuation	All my sentences begin with a capital letter and end with a period. I have used other punctuation correctly.	Most of my sentences begin with a capital and end with a period, but I forgot a few times.	I forgot to use capitals to start my sentences and did not always end with a period.		
Spelling	I re-read my writing carefully and checked my spelling to make sure it was correct.	I re-read my writing. I made some mistakes with my spelling.	I did not re-read my writing. I made a lot of spelling mistakes.		

Make a comment on what you can do to improve next time.

Teacher comment:

Figure 8.13: Rubric for writing exposition

Rubrics

Rubrics provide a way of gathering information for both teachers and students. Carefully designed rubrics can support the learner in understanding what is required as well as continue to assist them in the process of reflecting on their efforts. Rubrics help to ensure that the teacher and the student both understand the assessment task before beginning, and therefore both can share their thoughts on the task in a productive way.

Features of rubrics include:
- A focus on and definition of a quality performance
- A description of measurable criteria
- Development "up front" when the writing assignment is given
- Involvement of the students in construction
- Provision of an opportunity to plan and set goals.

The rubric in Figure 8.13 is designed to both assess and support learners in the writing of an exposition. It involves students and teacher in the assessment of the writing. Further, it involves students in reflecting on their "score" and deciding on some actions for their next piece of writing in order to demonstrate what they have learned from this experience. The teacher's role is to support or clarify what the student has written in the goal-setting phase of the rubric. The completed rubric needs to be made available to students when they next engage in a similar writing experience. Without the follow-up stage, a rubric can become a simple scoring mechanism that does little to engage students in reflecting deeply on their efforts.

The checklist in Figure 8.14 might be more appropriate for some students. While similar to the rubric, the checklist requires students to show examples of certain features of their writing.

Retelling

Retelling is a strategy that requires students to predict the content of an unseen text, read the text, and then retell it in their own words. As such it involves reading, writing, and listening and talking. It is an engaging activity, but is also an excellent assessment tool. Evidence of a students' reading comprehension can be gathered in addition to data on various aspects of their writing.

Procedure for a retelling

- Prepare a short fiction or factual text at independent reading level. One page is ideal.
- Decide on the purpose for using this strategy and therefore the text selected.

- Prepare a copy of the text selected for each student. Fold or staple so only the heading is visible.
- Begin by reading the title and asking the students to write a prediction of what the text will be about. Ask them to list words and phrases that you would expect to see in this text. Share predictions in small groups or pairs.
- Reveal the text and ask the students to follow the text as the teacher reads.
- Ask students to re-read the text silently with the purpose of understanding the text.
- Specify the audience and purpose of the retelling. Ask students to put the text away and retell the text in writing. This should be done quickly.
- Form pairs and share retellings with the purpose of students comparing and contrasting the retelling.
- Finally, ask the students to re-read the text and comment on the accuracy of their retelling.

The areas for assessment will vary as you use this strategy throughout the year, and a rubric may also be used alongside this rich activity to focus on particular aspects of writing within the retelling. The example in the following cameo describes Matthew in Grade 3 using a factual text.

Checklist for Exposition Writing

Name: _____ Date: _____

My Exposition	Yes/No	Example from My Writing
My exposition has a statement of position.		
I have stated my arguments clearly.		
I concluded my position statement.		
I have used complex sentences.		
I have used some technical language.		
Next time I write an exposition, I will:		

Figure 8.14: Checklist for writing exposition

Cameo: Factual Text and a Grade 3 Student

The following is the factual text read by Matthew.

Preserve Our Rainforest

Two hundred years ago Australia had large expanses of rainforest—lush areas of tall, densely packed trees—home to many unusual creatures.

However, the early settlers who followed Captain Cook, cleared and destroyed vast sections of this rainforest. They cleared land so they could farm, run cattle, and grow crops. They also destroyed much rainforest by logging the rich, red cedar trees which were wanted by furniture makers. Gradually our rainforest started to disappear—now there is not much left.

Australia must realise that the rainforest which remains must be preserved; clearing for farming and logging for timber must stop now before all our rainforest is destroyed. Many animals need the rainforest to survive; the cuscus and tree kangaroo live only in the rainforest. What will happen to them if we don't stop the destruction of our jungles? The government should preserve all rainforest as national parks so that all Australians, now and in the future, may enjoy their beauty (Brown and Cambourne 1987, 38).

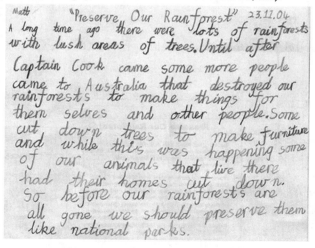

Figure 8.15: Retelling by Matthew, Grade 3

Name: Matt

Criteria	3	2	1	Student	Teacher
Accurate retelling	I did a good retelling and included all the main ideas in sequence. I also had a lot of detail in my retelling.	I did a good retelling and included most of the main ideas but I left some out. I left out a lot of the details.	My retelling did not include all the main ideas in sequence. I did not include any details.	2	
Spelling and punctuation	I have used correct spelling and punctuation. All my sentences begin with a capital and end with a full stop and I have used other punctuation correctly.	Most of my sentences begin with a capital and end with a full stop but I forgot a few times. I have made some mistakes with my spelling.	I forgot to use capitals to start my sentences and did not always end with a full stop. I have made too many mistakes with my spelling.	3	
Listening skills	I was a good listener when the teacher and my partner were speaking. I know what my partner's retelling sounded like and I followed the teacher's directions.	I did not listen carefully all the time when the teacher and my partner were speaking. I am not sure what my partner's retelling sounded like. I did not follow all of the directions.	I did not listen to my teacher or my partner. I do not know what my partner's retelling sounded like. I did not follow the directions given.	3	
Handwriting	My writing uses joined letters and I have good letter shape, size and slope all of the time.	I did not use joined letters and good letter shape, size and slope all of the time.	I did not use joined letters and good letter shape, size and slope.	3	
			TOTAL	11	

Student comment—
I can improve.... I can improve by putting some more details in my writing. I can improve this by rembering more things and not wasting time rubbing out.

Figure 8.16: Rubric for retelling by Matthew, Grade 3

Teacher

You have done a good retelling, Matt. I agree that you could include some more details that are important to the meaning. You will achieve this goal by using the reading time and reading carefully for meaning. I will also help you work on this when we are doing Reciprocal Teaching. I agree that lots of rubbing out wastes writing time, especially in a draft piece of writing. Well done!

Figure 8.17: Teacher response to Matthew's comments in his rubric

Proofreading

Proofreading activities provide a great deal of information about a student's writing and spelling skills. Below we discuss two approaches, "Peer Proofreading" and "Read and Spell." Peer proofreading is an excellent strategy to develop and assess proofreading skills, and Read and Spell is a spelling strategy that uses the proofreading skills of the student. The focus of Read and Spell is on assessing spelling strategies in use and developing a range of spelling strategies in addition to assessing and practicing proofreading skills.

Peer Proofreading

Peer Proofreading is an ideal strategy to use throughout the year to assess students' progress. It provides teachers with opportunities to focus on aspects of students' writing and proofreading that may not be observed by examining students' drafts and finished products alone. Peer Proofreading is an open-ended assessment strategy that requires students to proofread first-draft writing of unknown peers. During Peer Proofreading, the teacher carefully observes and records the problem-solving processes students go through as they try to correct the perceived errors in the given texts. As teachers observe the Peer Proofreading process, they ask questions and occasionally give prompts to ensure that students reveal as much of their control over the conventions and features of language as possible.

Peer Proofreading is not an appropriate strategy for very young children who are not yet proficient readers and writers, have not developed a strong sense of audience for their writing, and have not yet learned to work together cooperatively. These children are learning to read and write, however; so during the process of modeled writing, teachers may want to demonstrate the steps they go through as they proofread and edit their own writing. This modeling can then serve as a precursor for students to move more comfortably into Peer Proofreading at a later stage.

During Peer Proofreading, students typically focus on the following:

- Layout/formatting
- Spelling
- Punctuation/capitalization
- Grammar
- Genre features
- Penmanship/letter formation.

The focus varies according to the age of the student, the purpose of the task, and the contextual demands of the situation.

Peer Proofreading provides a "window" into students' current working models of conventions. What students do and say demonstrates what they know about the reading-writing connection and how they use what they know to make meaning with written language. In light of such information, it is therefore possible for teachers to make judgments about what students need to learn in the future. The purposes for Peer Proofreading include:

- Helping identify and understand the language knowledge, behaviors, and processes that students engage in when making sense of print composed by others
- Providing a clear indication of:
  - whether or not students view the primary reason for writing as a way of communicating logical, meaningful ideas to an audience
  - what strategies students already use, particularly with regard to spelling and punctuation
  - why students decide to use particular language knowledge for particular language tasks
  - how successful they are in their use of that language knowledge
  - what students need to know in order to progress as language users to gain direction for future planning.

Phase 1: Preparation for Peer Proofreading

Phase 1 consists of collecting two to five pieces of first draft writing from students who are in a grade level similar to the one you teach. Be sure to get the students' permission to use the pieces, particularly if you choose drafts from your own grade level. The number you chose should depend on the length of the pieces. Check that all pieces contain some errors. Type the drafts exactly as they are and make photocopies of both the handwritten and the typed versions.

Phase 2: Modeling Peer Proofreading

You may wish to model Peer Proofreading during a mini-lesson for either the whole class or a small group. Begin by showing students the handwritten and typed versions of the piece of writing you are going to proofread. Tell them which version you have chosen to work with and explain why. Read the piece aloud.

Next, go back and begin re-reading slowly, thinking aloud as you go. Stop on certain parts that you think need "fixing up." Explain why you are having problems with these parts, and show how you are going to fix them. When you have edited each trouble spot, read it again to be sure you are satisfied with your revision.

Model different strategies as you go, such as looking around the room for spelling of words, using a dictionary or other reference book as necessary, asking yourself questions such as, "What is the writer/What am I trying to say here? Does that sound better/make better sense now? Does that spelling/ punctuation/capitalization look right?" and asking for help or confirmation of certain changes or ideas.

When you have finished proofreading the entire piece, go back and read it all the way through. Invite questions and comments from the students about the process and the piece itself. If students suggest additional improvements to the piece, incorporate them at this time.

Phase 3: Introducing Peer Proofreading

1. Present a student with the first set of texts you have chosen. While showing the handwritten version, say, "This was written by a student who's in the same grade that you're in." Show the student the typed version and say, "This is the same story/text typed up exactly as Kim wrote it, but it's been done on the computer."
2. Read the text aloud, inviting the student to read with you whenever he or she can.
3. Ask the student to choose between the handwritten and the typed version and say, "Have a look at Kim's draft. Is there anything that doesn't look or sound quite right? Can you help her to fix it up? What needs changing?" Probe with questions and comments such as:
   - Can you fix up the spelling?
   - Put a circle around the words/phrases that you think need fixing up. Why does [say the word/phrase] need fixing? Can you write it the way you think it should go?
4. Keep going in this way until the student seems to have finished, then ask, "What else does Kim need to know about in her piece? What else would you tell her to do?"

Use the following probes if you think you will get more information:
- Are there any words that need to begin with a capital letter?
- Did Kim use the correct punctuation?
- Do you understand what Kim is trying to say in this piece?
- Is this an interesting/informative/amusing piece? How do you know?

Ask the student to circle anything identified from the above probes, then ask, "What should happen to that circled part?" Tell the student: "Re-write it the way you think it should be written."

Figure 8.18 is an example of what the child did and then the changes made after engaging in Peer Proofreading and Figure 8.19 is an analysis of this student's work.

Before Peer Proofreading:

Zak, Year 2 November 5

Draft 1:

It was Tuesday and the dad was havn a snak and he lokt out the windows. Thar were all kins of culrd frogs on their lile pads and the frogs wer comng aron the door and the windows and the dads her flyd up and he went o no! Its a frog etak! The dad had to get thos frogs out of their fast! But how???

After Peer Proofreading:

It was Tuesday and the dad was having a snack and he looked out the windows. There were all kinds of colored frogs on their lily pads and they were coming around the door and the windows. The dad's hair flew up and he went 'Oh no! It's a frog attack!!' The dad had to get those frogs out of there fast! But how?

Figure 8.18: Zak's writing before and after Peer Proofreading

Name: Zak C.   **Date:** November 5

What the student knows	What the student needs to work on
Use of capital letters Day of the week Beginning of a sentence	Indent to show paragraph beginnings
Use and purpose of exclamation and question marks	Sentences • where to begin and end • variety • length • combinations
Spelling of frequently used words	Grammar: possessives; there/their; flew instead of "flyd"
How to use environmental print for conventional spelling (Tuesday, door, windows)	Mechanics: quotation marks; capital letters within quotations

Figure 8.19: Zak's writing analysis

Phase 4: Follow-up

You may find it necessary to model the strategy again for students, especially if they have not used it in a while and need reminding. As an alternative, you can conduct peer proofreading in a group context and then interview students afterwards. This saves time but is not as informative. Another thing you can do is ask students to proofread a piece that they wrote themselves a few months before. This helps them see their progress, both as writers and as proofreaders.

It is vital for teachers to take on the role of participant/observer from time to time, observing students in action while asking probing questions. By watching and asking, teachers are able to tap into students' processes and get insights that are otherwise inaccessible to them.

Once students have begun to acquire the skills of proofreading, it can then be used to teach spelling and make links to the students' writing on a more complex level. Use peer proofreading several times during the year so that you can record trends and improvements in student profiles.

Read and Spell Strategy

Read and Spell is an example of a strategy that uses proofreading to teach and assess spelling.

Phase 1: Preparation

A good proofreading activity reflects the current spelling behaviors, which are observable in the classroom. Keep a list of the kinds of errors you observe in students' writing over the week. Use the list to construct this proofreading activity. Write a short passage containing the errors that you have observed. These errors will become the focus of the lesson.

Phase 2: Check the Passage

Make sure the writing you have constructed is as authentic as possible. The context in which spelling is demonstrated is important because spelling is a tool for writing, not an isolated skill or exercise. When preparing the proofreading text, make certain the proofreading errors are appropriate in kind and number for the students to experience success, particularly in the early phase of using this strategy. Too many errors will detract from the planned teaching points. Use between six and ten errors, all of which have a specific point based on class or group needs. For example, you might want to focus on plurals, such as adding -s , -ies, or -es. Later you can include aspects of punctuation and grammar. An example of such a passage is shown in Figure 8.20.

A Trip to the Zoo

On Tuesday I went to Taronga Zoo with my class.

First we had morning tea and then went to the bird show. My favret bird was the Black Cockatoo. I liked it because of the noise it made. I also likt the peacocks but their tale feathers lookt a bit funny.

We saw many anamals and birds. The spider monkeys and the seals were fun to watch.

after lunch we made our way back to the bus and went back to scool. I had

lots of fun.

Figure 8.20: Sample proofreading text

Phase 3: The Teaching Process

The teaching process can be a half-hour lesson or three mini-lessons, as described below. If engagement is difficult for the group, opt for the three ten-minute sessions to keep the lesson short and focused.

Day 1:

10 minutes: Students proofread the piece and "have a go" at the correct spelling. You read the passage and say, "I want you to listen and follow on your page while I read the text. Now I want you to read this passage carefully and look for any spelling errors. When you find an incorrect spelling, put a circle around that word and 'have a go' at spelling the word correctly. If you have any trouble reading any of the words, just ask me."

Day 2:

10 minutes: Typically there will be six to ten errors. Have volunteers come out and write the words identified as errors on the board. Begin with the first word. Say, "You knew 'different' was spelled incorrectly. Do you think you know how to spell 'different'? Can you write it on the whiteboard?"

Check the spelling. If it is correct, praise the student. If not, put a check mark over the letters that are correct.

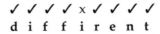

$$\checkmark \; \checkmark \; \checkmark \; \checkmark \; x \; \checkmark \; \checkmark \; \checkmark \; \checkmark$$
$$\text{d} \quad \text{i} \quad \text{f} \quad \text{f} \quad \text{i} \quad \text{r} \quad \text{e} \quad \text{n} \quad \text{t}$$

Say, "That is a great try, but there is a letter that needs changing. Look at all the letters you got correct! Would you like to have another go or will we ask someone to help?"

Once the word is correct, you can ask, "How did you know how to spell that word?" This is the key to the activity. The goal is to have the student articulate how he or she got to the spelling of the word so that the other students see the range of spelling strategies that are available to use. In the early stages you may have to do some modeling to help the students get the language to talk about their spelling. This will develop over time as you use this strategy. Gradually the students will become more articulate at describing the strategies they use, and the other students will hear new strategies. The table in Figure 8.21 gives an example of the typical responses.

Typical Student Response	Strategy in Use
I knew "beauty" and that helped me with the beginning of "beautiful."	Knowledge of words
I sounded "different" out.	Sounding out
I sounded out the parts of the word: diff/er/ent.	Syllabification
I looked on the word wall.	Reference to an authority
I knew a trick to spell "principal." I knew there was a "pal" in "principal."	Use of a mnemonic
I knew the rule that there is an "'i' before 'e' except after 'c' and when sounding like 'a' as in 'neighbor' and 'weigh.'"	Application of a rule
I knew that "there" is a homonym.	Knowledge of language
I knew it had to be "waste," not "waist," for the sentence to make sense.	Using meaning of words

Figure 8.21: Student responses to Read and Spell strategy

Students will often come up with unexpected strategies, and this gives the teacher an insight into how the student is approaching spelling. It is effective to ask more than one child how they got to the spelling of the word, but guard against the lesson dragging out.

Day 3:

10 minutes: Look at the words again and ask the group to classify or name them. Remember that there will be only six to ten words, but they are words you have selected so you will be prepared to help here. Say, "Look at this list of words that was in our proofreading task. Can anyone see a pattern in the words or a way to classify them?" A pattern, for example, might be using contractions, adding -ed, or adding -ing. Make sure you are clear on the categories before beginning so you can assist the students with accurate information. An example is shown in Figure 8.22.

favret	favorite	chunking
likt	liked	adding "-ed"
tale	tail	homophone
lookt	looked	adding "-ed"
anamals	animals	chunking
scool	school	visual

Figure 8.22: Sample of listing and categorizing spelling patterns

Once the words have been grouped and classified, the final step is for the group to take a closer look at a piece they are writing and look for examples of the spelling discussed, such as contractions or adding "-ed." This last step of taking the students back to their writing is critical because the goal is to transfer this extremely focused learning to their writing, and the link to writing must be made explicit.

FINAL COMMENTS

In recent times the purposes of assessment have come to encompass many things. With a growth in state-wide and national testing, assessment is now often used to compare students across districts, states, and the nation. This often detracts from the kinds of assessment tools and strategies that will impact on better teaching and learning. We therefore believe that teachers must design their assessments to not only identify what their students have learned but also to learn what their students need to learn next. In this way the assessment process will inform their teaching. To this end, teachers need to be cognizant of the range of assessment tools and strategies available to them so they can select those that are rigorous and will provide valid information. Effective assessment should:

- inform teachers so they can guide students to the next stage of learning
- provide information for teachers to better understand the students they are teaching
- provide information so that teachers can articulate their knowledge of the students they teach
- help teachers reflect on the approaches and strategies they are using to teach writing.

Chapter 9: Teacher Response to Assessment Data

After collecting all this information, teachers need a way to reflect on what they see and on the data they collect. In others words, teachers need to respond appropriately to the needs of individual students based on this information. Regie Routman says, "If we make an assessment and don't use it to move teaching and learning forward, the assessment is largely a waste of time" (2002, 107).

RODGERS' MODEL FOR REFLECTION

The area of reflection on teaching and learning is a complex one. The work of Carol Rodgers is helpful in understanding the complexity of reflection for teachers and students. Rodgers suggests how teachers "through a structured process of reflection, become present—to see student learning: to discern, differentiate, and describe the elements of learning, to analyze the learning and to respond, as John Dewey says, 'intelligently'" (2002, 231). Rodgers' model offers a process of reflection that will take us to "intelligent" action. Through reflection, teacher response can sometimes be immediate and sometimes it will involve further thinking and planning.

The four parts of Rodgers' model are:

- Presence in Experience (learning to see)
- Description of Experience (learning to describe and differentiate)
- Analysis of Experience (learning to think from multiple perspectives and form multiple explanations)
- Experimentation (learning to take "intelligent action").

When thinking about writing and the assessment strategies we have suggested they might be connected to the Rodgers' model in the following way:

- Presence in Experience: Observe, take field notes, use rubrics, and assess writing samples.

- Description of Experience: Consider the context / problem
- Analysis of Experience: List teaching strategies and experiences across the stages of the writing process; explore multiple perspectives and explanations
- Experimentation: Take "intelligent" action on findings.

AN EXAMPLE OF REFLECTION

- Presence in Experience: My Grade 4 students have been writing narratives.
- Description of Experience: I have observed that for many of my students they have not identified an audience and purpose for their writing. Their early attempts are rambling and lack imagery (descriptive language).
- Analysis of Experience: I think that they may need help in understanding that "stories" or narratives have strong characters, interesting settings, and exciting plots in order to engage readers.
- Experimentation: Figure 9.1 shows a grid that responds to the description and analysis of the experience.

Before Writing	During Writing	After Writing
Read some well-chosen narratives over several days. With each example discuss the audience and purpose for the writing. First day: ask students to make notes about the characters in the text as they listen, thinking about the author's intended audience and purpose. Next day: the settings. Next day: the plot. Form a circle and discuss findings each day. Teacher notes the findings on a chart.	Use the findings to make a checklist or scaffold. Provide students with the scaffold to refer to when writing with some key points about the structure of a narrative and helpful questions to keep their focus on the characters, setting, and plot in relation to the audience and purpose for the writing.	Provide an opportunity for students to share their writing in groups of 3. As two of the students listen to each piece have them make notes about the characters, setting, and plot in relation to the audience and purpose identified by the writer. Have students reflect by using a rubric designed to match the checklist / scaffold that they used when writing. Make sure the rubric has a section where the students can comment on what they can do next time to continue to improve.

Figure 9.1: Format for teacher reflection on student writing

ASSESSING TEACHING STRATEGIES

The other time when assessment must take place is when we reflect on what we do as teachers. In reference to the Reflection Cycle (Rodgers 2002) this will involve *Analysis of Experience.* A good place to start is to think deeply about the key strategies described in Chapter 5 used in relation to the class or group of students. It may mean making substantial changes to how we teach in order to ensure that needs are met.

The grid in Figure 9.2 summarizes the key teaching strategies suggested for the teaching of writing and suggests assessment strategies that could be employed. Further, it offers a set of reflective questions for the teacher. These are suggestions as to the things the teacher may need to keep in mind in the day-to-day teaching of writing. The quality of the questions we ask ourselves will improve as we become more reflective. Critical reflection that leads to "intelligent action" is one of the key strategies for the teacher of writing. The big question might be: "Is what I am currently doing in modeled writing/shared writing/guided writing impacting positively on all students' writing and learning about writing?"

Whole-school approaches to organizing writing workshops can support students in developing as writers. A whole-school plan for the teaching of writing will serve to clarify beliefs across grades related to approaches used in writing. The goal is not that every teacher will teach the same way but that they have a common approach to teaching strategies and assessment that will be supportive of each student's learning. Simple actions such as the development of an agreed whole-school proofreading guide (see example in Appendix 9) can save time and confusion as students move through the grades. Further, defining what you mean by the writing processes to develop shared meaning is an important step. The aim of a whole-school plan is to allow the child to move easily through the grades, building on the skills that they are acquiring. A good starting point in any school may well be to consider the words of Don Holdaway: "Learning to read and write ought to be one of the most joyful and successful of human undertakings" (1979, 11).

Strategy	Description of Strategy	Opportunities for Assessment	Reflective Questions
		Assessment of Key Teaching Strategies for Writing	
Modeled Writing	The teacher writes and "thinks aloud." The short, focused lesson is based on observed needs.	• Teacher observation • Interaction with students • Analysis of written response (when appropriate).	• Were the students engaged? • Was the lesson focused on observed needs? • Did I achieve my purpose for the lesson?
Shared Writing	• Also referred to as "joint construction." • Teacher plans the writing and holds the pen, but unlike modeled writing, involves the students in construction.	• Observation of student involvement • Observation of contributions and suggestions made by the students • Interaction with students.	• Were the students engaged? • Did I involve all the students? • Did the lesson meet the students' needs? • Which students have the understanding to move to independent writing? • What was the application of skills demonstrated?
Guided Writing	• Carefully planned small group instruction to meet observed needs or to extend • Involves student conferencing.	• Anecdotal records • Teacher checklist • Analysis of writing samples • Peer assessment and self-evaluation.	• Are the sessions meeting the observed needs? • What level of support is required? • Am I extending the students? • What spelling strategies are the students using?
Independent Writing	• Writing for a clearly identified audience and purpose.	• Analysis of writing (at word, sentence, and text levels) • Observation of helping circle (editing) • Rubrics and student self-evaluation • Teacher and / or student checklists.	• Are the students enjoying writing? • Do they perceive audience and purpose for their writing and write for that audience and purpose? • Can they use this knowledge and select the correct genre for their writing? • Do the students follow up suggestions made in the helping circle? • Are they applying the skills taught in modeled and shared writing? • What skills are they using (spelling, proofreading, and so on)? • What scaffolds and resources are the students using when writing?

Figure 9.2: Assessing teacher writing strategies

Professional Development Activity: Analyzing Writing

Activity Preparation

1. Collect draft writing samples (must not be in published form) from your grade. Make sure each sample has the date and the child's full name.
2. Before the meeting, sort the class writing samples according to achievement levels. For example, the Grade 3 teacher would group together any writing considered to be underachieving for that grade, those pieces achieving at Grade 3, and those achieving beyond the grade expectations.
3. Teachers bring:
   - Writing samples that have been grouped
   - Any resources that are used in the grade that would be useful reference material.

Process

1. Discuss criteria used for selecting writing:

Ask each teacher to discuss the criteria they used to group the writing samples. The workshop facilitator should note what they say and read the list back to the group. Typically, a range of criteria is used that is inconsistent across the group of teachers.

Question: If we all use different criteria to assess writing in our grades, what impact will this have on our students?

2. Exploring audience and purpose:

Ask each teacher to select one piece of writing at a time and state the audience and the purpose for that piece as the teacher intended.

Now look at the writing and state the audience and purpose from the student's point of view.

Annotating Writing Samples

1. Return to the list of criteria used by the group and together create a single list that teachers agree would be useful in assessing draft writing. Organize the list by the categories of word, sentence, and text level.
2. Re-sort the writing according to these criteria.
3. Annotate one piece of writing (in pairs) for the grade you are working at. Join another pair and describe the decisions made.
4. As a whole group discuss learning, issues, and concerns.

Chapter 9

Concluding Thoughts

Throughout this book, we have shared both our beliefs about the teaching of writing and our experiences of working with young writers and their teachers. Our examples come from the classrooms where we have been inspired by what is possible when teachers and their students become aware of the role of audience and purpose when writing. This book has aimed to bring these observations together with what we know about writing as a social multidimensional practice through the many cameos and practical strategies.

We believe strongly that quality teaching is underpinned by sound theory. Therefore, we have also shared many theoretical underpinnings about writing itself, its connection to language—particularly to reading—as well as the research about the effective teaching of writing. Understanding the nexus between theory and practice, we believe, provides a solid foundation for the teaching and assessing of writing, and for this reason we have included professional development activities throughout the book. We have used these activities with many teachers over the years and have observed them learn and grow as teachers of writing. We hope that this same learning occurs for all who read our book. We only wish we could be there to observe you all!

Appendices

1. Teacher Checklist—The Process of Writing
2. Teacher Checklist—The Product of Writing
3. Check Your Own Writing—A Student Writing Checklist for Beginning Writers
4. Student Checklist to Guide Self-assessment
5. Student Writing Checklist
6. Rubric for Exposition Writing
7. Checklist for Exposition Writing
8. Have-a-Go Sheet
9. Proofreading Guide

Teacher Checklist—The Process of Writing

Name _____ Grade _____ Date _____

The Writing Process	Comment
Focusing Has the student identified an audience and purpose for the writing? Has the student selected an appropriate genre? Has the student engaged in any planning before commencing to write? Has the student collected and organized information? Has the student maintained the focus?	
Composing Is the student willing to write? Does the student have spelling strategies to create a text? Does the student have knowledge of text structure to create a text?	
Editing Is the student willing to edit? Can the student adopt the stance of a reader to identify points where meaning is lost or information is incomplete? Can the student refine meaning and make choices between different ways of saying the same thing?	
Proofreading Can the student identify non-standard spelling and grammar? Can the student correct identified errors? Is the student applying a range of spelling strategies? Is the student using punctuation, sentence, and paragraph conventions appropriately?	
Publishing Can the student think back to the audience and purpose and determine the form of publishing that is appropriate?	

Teacher Checklist—The Product of Writing

Name _____ Grade _____ Date _____

Writing Product	Comment
Topic Is the topic appropriate to the audience? Is there sufficient information or are there things the reader still needs to know? Are the ideas or events properly sequenced? Is there coherence (related to the genre)? Are the ideas original? Are they presented originally? (Retelling and modeling may be encouraged, but copying the work of others—plagiarism—should be discouraged.)	
Audience Who is the audience? Is the subject matter appropriate to the audience? Is the language appropriate to the audience? Is the presentation appropriate to the audience? • spelling • punctuation • grammar • handwriting • layout Has the writing been edited and proofread? Are spelling, punctuation, and grammar appropriate?	
Purpose What was the purpose of the writing? Was it achieved? Did the writing entertain, inform, persuade, make comparisons, record observations, clarify thinking, predict, or hypothesize, depending on the genre?	
Genre Is the student in control of the text form? Is the control full or partial? Can the student structure and sustain a narrative, report, letter, or play, or does the structure break down? Which genre has the student made use of?	

Check Your Own Writing

Name _____ Date _____

1. Spelling

Circle the words that you think may be spelled incorrectly.

Look for the correct spelling:
- on the walls
- in a dictionary
- in your word list.

2. Punctuation

Check that you have used capital letters and periods.

Check that commas, question marks, and quotation marks are in the correct place.

3. Does your writing make sense?

Read your writing out loud.

Is there anything you need to add or to take out?

Student Checklist to Guide Self-Assessment

Name _____ Date _____

Purpose of my writing: _____

Audience for my writing: _____

Genre selected: _____

My writing makes sense.

☐ I have read my writing out loud.

☐ I have checked to see if there is anything I need to add or to take out.

Spelling

☐ I have circled the words that I need to check for correct spelling.

I have looked for the correct spelling:
☐ on the word walls
☐ in a dictionary
☐ in my word list.

Punctuation

☐ I have checked that I have used capital letters and periods.

☐ I have checked that I have used commas, question marks, and quotation marks correctly.

☐ I am ready for a conference.

Student Writing Checklist

Name: _____ Date: _____

1. Does your writing make sense? 　Hints: • Who is the audience for this piece of writing? • What was the purpose of the writing? • Do the events or facts follow each other in proper order or are some parts jumbled? • Are there any parts you need to add or cut?	
2. Is your spelling correct? Proofread your writing and circle the words that you think may be spelled incorrectly. 　Hint: • To check your spelling, use a ruler to uncover your text and read line-by-line, paying attention to each word. To find the correct spelling, refer to a dictionary, word lists in the room, or a book where you remember seeing the word.	
3. Is each sentence a complete thought that begins with a capital letter and ends with a period? 　Hint: • Go back and read your writing out loud quietly to check that the whole piece sounds right. You will be able to hear where the sentences begin and end.	
4. Is your punctuation correct? Check that you have used capital letters and that commas, periods, question marks, and quotation marks are in the correct place. 　Hints: • Have you used a capital letter for people's names or places? • Are there sentences that ask a question? Do they end with question marks? • Do you have characters talking in your writing? Have you used quotation marks? • Is the paragraphing correct?	
5. Is your use of grammar correct? 　Hint: • Are nouns, pronouns, and verbs in agreement? • Is your use of tense correct and consistent?	
6. Is your handwriting clear and are your letters well formed? 　Hint: • Neat handwriting will help whoever reads your writing to enjoy and understand what you have written.	

Rubric for Exposition Writing—Grade 2

Name: _____ Date: _____

Criteria	3	2	1	Student	Teacher
Structure	I used the correct structure for my exposition. • I began with a clear opening statement. • I wrote several reasons for or against the topic. • I ended my writing by stating my position.	I did not include all the structures needed for an exposition.	I did not use the correct structure when I wrote my exposition.		
Punctuation	All my sentences begin with a capital letter and end with a period. I have used other punctuation correctly.	Most of my sentences begin with a capital and end with a period, but I forgot a few times.	I forgot to use capitals to start my sentences and did not always end with a period.		
Spelling	I re-read my writing carefully and checked my spelling to make sure it was correct.	I re-read my writing. I made some mistakes with my spelling.	I did not re-read my writing. I made a lot of spelling mistakes.		

Make a comment on what you can do to improve next time.

Teacher comment:

Checklist for Exposition Writing

Name: _____ Date: _____

My Exposition	Yes/No	Example from My Writing
My exposition has a statement of position.		
I have stated my arguments clearly.		
I concluded by reinforcing my position statement.		
I have used complex sentences.		
I have used some technical language.		

Next time I write an exposition, I will:

Have-a-Go Sheet

This list belongs to: _____

First Attempt at Writing	Have a Go	Correct Spelling

Proofreading Guide

Mark	Meaning	Example
⋀	Add a letter, word or other material.	We went ⋀ the park.
—	Change to a capital letter.	On <u>s</u>aturday we went to the zoo.
◯	Add a period.	The zoo was fun◯
[	Start a new paragraph.	[After lunch we went home.
⬯	Check spelling.	We saw lots of (anamals.)
———	Check word.	Jan and <u>me</u>
‿	Close up space.	Thought‿ful

References

Ahlberg, Janet and Allan Ahlberg. 1986. *The Jolly Postman or Other People's Letters.* London: Puffin Books.

Anthony, Robert J., Terry D. Johnson, Norma L. Mickelson, and Alison Preece. 1991. *Evaluating Literacy: A Perspective for Change.* Portsmouth, NH: Heinemann.

Bean, Wendy. 1998. "Spelling Across the Grades" in *Getting Started.* Sydney, Australia: Primary English Teaching Association.

Bean, Wendy. 2000. *Ways to Teach Spelling.* Sydney, Australia: Primary English Teaching Association.

Bean, Wendy and Chrystine Bouffler. 1987. *Spell by Writing.* Rozelle, NSW, Australia: Primary English Teaching Association and Portsmouth, NH: Heinemann.

Bean, Wendy and Chrystine Bouffler. 1997. *Spelling: An Integrated Approach.* Melbourne, Australia: Eleanor Curtain Publishing. Reprinted by Stenhouse as *Read, Write, Spell,* 1997.

Bear, Donald R., Marcia Invernizzi, Shane R. Templeton, and Francine Johnston. 2003. *Words Their Way: Word Study for Phonics, Vocabulary, and Spelling Instruction,* 3/e. Upper Saddle River, NJ: Prentice Hall.

Bedford, Sybille. 1974. *Aldous Huxley: A Biography.* New York, NY: Knopf/Random House. Reissued by Ivan R. Dee Publisher, 2002.

Brown, Hazel and Brian Cambourne. 1987. *Read and Retell: A Strategy for the Whole Language/Natural Learning Classroom.* Melbourne, Australia: Methuen and Portsmouth, NH: Heinemann, 1990.

Butler, Andrea and Jan Turbill. 1984. *Towards a Reading-Writing Classroom.* Rozelle, NSW, Australia: Primary English Teaching Association and Portsmouth, NH: Heinemann, 1987.

Every effort has been made to include complete Australian and U. S. publication information.

Calkins, Lucy. 1983. *Lessons from a Child: On the Teaching and Learning of Writing*. Portsmouth, NH: Heinemann.

Cambourne, Brian. 1988. *The Whole Story: Natural Learning and the Acquisition of Literacy*. Auckland, New Zealand: Scholastic New Zealand.

Cambourne, Brian and Jan Turbill. 1987. *Coping with Chaos*. Rozelle, NSW, Australia: Primary English Teaching Association and Portsmouth, NH: Heinemann.

Clay, Marie M. 1975. *What Did I Write? Beginning Writing Behaviour*. Portsmouth, NH: Heinemann Educational Books.

Conner, P. 2003. "The Development of Student Writing through the Use of the Six Traits of Writing and Self-Assessment." Unpublished dissertation, Hamline University, Saint Paul, MN.

Croft, Cedric. 1997. *Write to Spell in Primary Classrooms*. New Zealand Council for Educational Research and ACER: Language and Literacy Number 11, page 1.

Culham, Ruth. 2003. *6+1 Traits of Writing: The Complete Guide (Grades 3 and Up)*. New York, NY: Scholastic Professional Books.

Day, E. 1999. "Assessment Criteria of Grade 2 Teachers." Honours thesis, University of Wollongong, Australia.

Delpit, Lisa. 1988. "The Silenced Dialogue: Power and Pedagogy in Education other People's Children." *Harvard Educational Review*. Volume 58, number 3, pages 280-298.

Derewianka, Beverly. 1990. *Exploring How Texts Work*. Sydney, Australia: Primary English Teaching Association.

Dumbrell, Laurel. 1997. *You Can Write—Here's Proof*. Parramatta, NSW, Australia: Talver.

Elbow, Peter. 1981. *Writing with Power: Techniques for Mastering the Writing Process*. London: Oxford and New York, NY: Oxford University Press.

Elbow, Peter. 2004. "Writing First!" *Educational Leadership*. Volume 62, number 2, pages 8-14.

Flower, Linda. 1979. "Writer-based Prose: A Cognitive Basis for Problems in Writing." *College English*. Volume 41, number 1, September, pages 19-37.

Fountas, Irene and Gay Su Pinnell. 2000. *Guiding Readers and Writers Grades 3-6: Teaching Comprehension, Genre, and Content Literacy*. Portsmouth, NH: Heinemann.

Fox, Mem and Judy Horacek. 2004. *Where Is the Green Sheep?* New York, NY: Harcourt Children's Books.

Fox, Mem and Lyn Wilkinson. 1993. *English Essentials: The Wouldn't-be-without-it Guide to Writing Well.* Melbourne, Australia: Macmillan.

Freire, Paolo. 1976. *Education: The Practice of Freedom.* London: Writers and Readers Publishing Cooperative.

Freire, Paolo. 1998. *Pedagogy of Freedom: Ethics, Democracy, and Civic Courage.* Lanham, MD: Rowman and Littlefield Publishers, Inc.

Graves, Donald. 1982. *Writing: Teachers and Children at Work.* Portsmouth, NH: Heinemann.

Graves, Donald. 2004. "What I Have Learned from Teachers of Writing." *Language Arts.* Volume 82, number 2, pages 88-94.

Halliday, M. A. K. 1969. "Relevant Models of Language." *Educational Review.* Volume 22, number 1, pages 26-37.

Harris, Pauline, Barbra McKenzie, Phil Fitzsimmons, and Jan Turbill. 2003. *Writing in the Primary School Years.* Tuggerah, NSW, Australia: Social Science Press.

Harste, Jerome C., Virginia A. Woodward, and Carolyn Burke. 1984. *Language Stories and Literacy Lessons.* Portsmouth, NH: Heinemann.

Harvey, Stephanie. 1998. *Nonfiction Matters: Reading, Writing, and Research in Grades 3-8.* Portland, ME: Stenhouse Publishers.

Harwayne, Shelley. 2000. *Lifetime Guarantees: Toward Ambitious Literacy Teaching.* Portsmouth, NH: Heinemann.

Harwayne, Shelley. 2001. *Writing through Childhood: Rethinking Process and Product.* Portsmouth, NH: Heinemann.

Holdaway, Don. 1979. *The Foundations of Literacy.* Auckland, New Zealand: Ashton Scholastic.

Hughes, Margaret and Dennis Searle. 2000. "Spelling and 'the Second R'." *Language Arts.* Volume 77, number 3, pages 203-208.

Jancola, Linda. (no date). "E.T. Story Starter." http://www.kent.k12.wa.us/staff/LindaJancola/6Trait/lessons/et.htm, accessed January 2005.

Kirby, Allan. (no date). "Creative Writing Process: A Step by Step Approach to Writing." http://www.nzcal.com/hp/adk/, accessed January 2005.

Kohn, Alfie. 1999. *The Schools Our Children Deserve: Moving Beyond Traditional Classrooms and "Tougher Standards."* Boston, MA: Houghton Mifflin.

Louden, William, Mary Rohl, Caroline Barratt-Pugh, Claire Brown, Trevor Cairney, Jess Elderfield, Helen House, Marion Meiers, Judity Ruvaukand, and Ken Rowe. 2005. "In Teachers' Hands: Effective Literacy Teaching Practices in the Early Years of Schooling. "A special edition of the *Australian Journal of Language and Literacy*. Volume 28, number 3, pages 171-255.

Luke, A. 1993. "The Social Construction of Literacy in the Primary School." In *Literacy, Learning and Teaching: Language as Social Practice in the Primary School*. Len Unsworth, editor. Melbourne, Australia: Palgrave Macmillan.

Macrorie, Ken. 1985. *Telling Writing*, 4/e. Montclair, NJ: Boynton/Cook Publishers.

Milne, A. A. 1926. *Winnie-the-Pooh*. London: Methuen.

Mooney, Margaret E. 2001. *Text Forms and Features: A Resource for Intentional Teaching*. Katonah, NY: Richard C. Owen Publishers, Inc.

Murray, Donald M. 1982. *Learning by Teaching: Selected Articles on Writing and Teaching*. Montclair, NJ: Boynton/Cook.

Polacco, Patricia. *Thank You, Mr. Falker*. 1998. New York, NY: Philomel Books.

Rodgers, Carol R. 2002. "Seeing Student Learning: Teacher Change and the Role of Reflection." *Harvard Educational Review*. Volume 72, number 2, Summer 2002, pages 230-253.

Routman, Regie. 2002. *Reading Essentials: The Specifics You Need to Teach Reading Well*. Portsmouth, NH: Heinemann.

Schimmel, Schim. 1994. *Dear Children of the Earth: A Letter from Home*. Minnesota: Creative Publishing International Inc./NorthWord Press.

Skinner, B. F. 1957. *Verbal Behavior*. Englewood Cliffs, NJ: Prentice Hall.

Smith, Frank. 1982. *Writing and the Writer*. London: Heinemann Primary.

Smith, Frank. 1983. "Reading Like a Writer." *Language Arts*. Volume 60, number 5, pages 558-567.

Spandel, Vicki. 2000. *Creating Writers: Linking Writing Assessment Instruction*, 3/e. New York: Addison Wesley/Longman.

Taylor, Barbara M., Michael Pressley, and P. David Pearson. 2002. *Research-Supported Characteristics of Teachers and Schools that Promote Reading Achievement*. Washington, DC: National Education Association.

Tierney, Robert and P. David Pearson. 1983. "Towards a Composing Model of Reading." *Language Arts*. Volume 60, number 5, pages 568-580.

Turbill, Jan, editor. 1982. *No Better Way to Teach Writing.* Rozelle, NSW, Australia: Primary English Teaching Association and Portsmouth, NH: Heinemann, 1995.

Turbill, Jan. 1983. *Now We Want to Write!* Rozelle, NSW, Australia: Primary English Teaching Association and Portsmouth, NH: Heinemann, 1995.

Turbill, Jan. 2003. "Exploring the Potential of the Digital Language Experience Approach in Australian Classrooms." *Reading Online.* Volume 6, number 7. http://www.readingonline.org/international/inter_index. asp?HREF=turbill7, accessed March 13, 2005.

U. S. Department of Education. 2001. Office of Educational Research and Improvement. National Center for Education Statistics. *The NAEP 1998 Technical Report,* NCES 2001-509, by Allen, N. L., J. R. Donoghue, and T. L. Schoeps. Washington, DC: National Center for Education Statistics.

Walshe, R. D., editor. 1981. *Donald Graves in Australia: Children Want to Write.* Rozelle, NSW, Australia: Primary English Teaching Association.

Walshe, R. D. 1982. *Every Child Can Write: Learning and Teaching Written Expression in the 80s.* Sydney, Australia: Primary English Teaching Association.

White, E. B. 1952. *Charlotte's Web.* London: Penguin Books. HarperCollins/ HarperTrophy, 1974.

Index